YACHTING
MONTHLY

200
SKIPPER'S TIPS

INSTANT SKILLS TO IMPROVE YOUR SEAMANSHIP

YACHTING MONTHLY

200

SKIPPER'S TIPS

INSTANT SKILLS TO IMPROVE YOUR SEAMANSHIP

Tom Cunliffe

FERNHURST
BOOKS

This edition first published in 2010 by John Wiley & Sons Ltd
Reprinted in 2013 by John Wiley & Sons Ltd
Reprinted in 2013 by Fernhurst Books Limited
62 Brandon Parade, Holly Walk, Leamington Spa, Warwickshire CV32 4JE
Tel: +44 (0) 1926 337488
www.fernhurstbooks.com

Library of Congress Cataloging-in-Publication Data

Cunliffe, Tom, 1947-
    Yachting monthly 200 skipper's tips : instant skills to improve your
seamanship / Tom Cunliffe.
        p. cm.
    Includes bibliographical references and index.
    ISBN 978-0-470-97288-5 (pbk.)
    1. Yachting. 2. Seamanship. 3. Navigation. I. Yachting
monthly and motor boating magazine.   II. Title.
    GV811.C873 2010
    797.1'24—dc22
                                                            2010028562

A catalogue record for this book is available from the British Library.

Set in 8/9 Humanist 777 BT Light by Thomson Digital, India
Printed in China through World Print

CONTENTS

PREFACE

Longer ago that I'd care to admit, the editor of *Yachting Monthly* asked me to pen a few tips for skippers and crews. I wasn't acknowledged as author of these early efforts, but I soon found I was delivering a group of them each month. I've never had proprietary rights to this page of goodies and I fully expected that it wouldn't last, but it kept right on going through the GPS revolution and the arrival of the reliable chart-plotter. Today, I still sit down once every four weeks to deliver these bite-sized chunks of information.

Writing tips isn't always the easiest of jobs. For a start, pitching the right level of reader expertise takes some thought. A jewel for one skipper might be blatantly obvious to another. Some perfectly competent people have no natural interest in electronics but feel that maybe they should. For them, a quick idea about checking a waypoint might save a lot of embarrassment. To a technophile whose greatest delight is pressing buttons and reading manuals, it's an insult to put it in the magazine. On the other side of the five-pound note, an old gaffer who uses rolling hitches and topsail halyard bends as matter of course may take amiss any offer of help in securing to a single bollard. He's right, of course, but I wonder how he'd get on peeling spinnakers on a dark, windy night.

Another pitfall for the tip-writer is the inevitable danger of repetition. After all, sailing is not exactly astrophysics. I often think there isn't much to it really, yet every time I go out there I discover a fresh slant on an old issue. After twenty years, a degree of saying what has been said can't be avoided, but at least I try to offer the nugget in a different way or from a new perspective.

Please bear all this in mind as you dip into this little book. Also, try to be kind to my old-fashioned insistence on referring to boats as 'she' and people as 'he' where only a personal pronoun will do. English is inadequate in this department, and no disrespect is intended to the ladies. I can't keep writing 'he or she', and the day I use 'their' for a single person will be the day they tip my last remains in the broad Atlantic.

I'm grateful to Wiley for coming up with the idea and to YM for giving us our head to get on with it. You may recognise some old friends or the tips may all be new to you, but, whoever you may be, I hope you find something useful.

Tom Cunliffe
June 2010

SEAMANSHIP

1 A QUESTION OF COURTESY

Not all boats that race are flat-out 'Grand Prix' jobs. Many a cruiser enjoys the odd weekend's sport with the local club. Such a boat could easily be taken for a cruiser, which on any other day she may well be. Today, however, she isn't flying an ensign, and this is the international sign that she's racing. As soon as she finishes or retires, she should hoist her ensign again so that her fellow competitors and anyone else around knows that she's no longer subject to the racing rules. Right now, those of us who are cruising might like to give her clear wind. It could be us one day.

No ensign? Then she's probably racing

2 WHOSE RIGHT OF WAY?

A useful aide-mémoire when crossing another vessel in daylight with both boats under power, is to ask yourself which of her side-lights you would be seeing if it were dark. A red (port) light would suggest that you are to take care, so stay out of her way. Green is for 'go', so if you see her starboard bow you can stand on carefully.

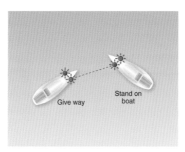

Picture the lights to work out who has right of way in daylight under power

3   IDENTIFYING A COLLISION RISK

Out at sea, collision risk is checked by ascertaining whether or not the vessel in question is maintaining a steady bearing relative to you. Initially, this is spotted by keeping your head still and seeing whether a distant ship remains in place over a particular stanchion, shroud, or other likely item. If it looks like a possibility but you are uncertain, you will take the ship's compass bearing, and keep checking as range closes. You might even use the electronic bearing line on your radar.

In confined waters, it is more convenient to note whether or not the other craft appears steady relative to its background. While difficult to prove mathematically, this old rule of thumb works every time unless the other craft is almost on the beach. If the other vessel stays in front of the same far-off field, chimney or parked car as you approach, you are on a collision heading, so watch out!

Line up the ship with a stanchion if there's nothing in the background to use as a reference

4   DIVER DOWN!

Learning all the code flags is no longer a part of any yachting syllabus, but every watchkeeper must be aware of the meaning of the 'A' flag. It says: "I have a diver down. Keep well clear at slow speed." Sometimes these flags are made of plywood, sometimes of fabric, but it is always dive boats that show them. Watch out for them and comply with their request. If you miss one, you could be responsible for causing a serious accident. Even if you don't hurt anyone, you'll get a well-deserved earful from the cox'n of the dive boat.

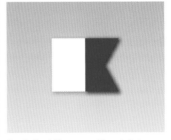

Be vigilant if you see Flag A flying

5 TURNING UP

The only certainty about how to make fast to a cleat is that there are a number of equally good ways of doing it. In deciding which to use, the questions to ask are:

- If I secure it like this, will it be impossible for the rope to come off by mistake?
- Will it also be impossible for the rope to jam up on the cleat?
- Have I put the turns on in such a way that, as I begin to take them off again, the rope can be surged under load if required?

Three 'yes' answers, and you've got it right. Notice that in the first picture **(Cleat 1)**, care is being taken that the second half of the initial turn on a poorly but typically aligned cleat cannot lock under load against the first half. **Cleat 2** shows a neat, safe job in progress, with figures of eight going on in a non-jammable way. **Cleat 3** shows a classic 'half a turn, two figures-of-eight and a final round turn' solution. Usually a winner, but if you're short of rope or the cleat isn't big enough, have no fear of using a locking hitch as in **Cleat 4**. These are not the only ways, though.

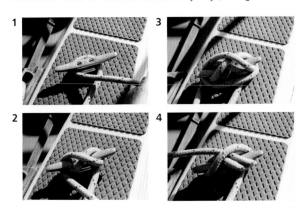

6 LOOK ALOFT

If you set your rig up yourself you may be completely confident in it but if it was left to anyone else to do, it's worth checking your pins and clevises before a passage. If you can't conveniently go aloft, rack the binoculars down to their shortest range, clean the lenses and take a serious look aloft. You'll be surprised at what you can see.

Use binoculars to check your rig

7   WHERE'S YOUR BALL?

We all know that we should hoist a black ball when we drop anchor, yet many of us neglect to do so. One reason for this is that the ball is often tucked behind a toolbox at the back of a locker and it's easy to 'forget' to go and get it. So why not stow it in the anchor locker where it'll always be to hand?

Stow your anchor ball in the chain locker and you'll always be able to find it

8   NEVER STOP COMMUNICATING

Any skipper can become so involved with the challenges of command that he or she forgets to keep the crew in the picture. It's as important for a briefing to include the basics of the coming passage as to explain where the life raft is and how to use the heads. As the miles roll along, morale is boosted if all hands are advised about progress. A man freezing in the cockpit will cope better if he knows the tide will turn in the next hour and that the gruesome sea state should soon begin to ease; an encouraging remark about there only being another 15 miles to go might save a mutiny. It sounds obvious, but it's often ignored.

A good skipper should keep his crew informed – it's a great way to boost morale

9   VIEW FROM THE BRIDGE

It's been said often enough, but it's easy to forget what the chaps on the big ships can't see. Here's an unusual view of the Solent, showing 'what the pilot saw' as a yacht scuttled under his bows a good quarter mile ahead. This one was quite safe as it happened, but if she'd been a bit closer and things had gone wrong for her, the people on the bridge wouldn't even have known they'd hit her.

What the pilot sees . . .

10   ONE FLAG WORTH KNOWING

The days when Yachtmasters had to learn all the signal flags are mercifully long past. However, the ability to recognise one or two of the signals remains a useful safety factor. The 'T' flag looks like a French ensign with the colours back to front. It means that the vessel flying it is engaged in pair trawling. Somewhere away on her beam will be her partner, and the consequences of finding yourself between them don't bear thinking about. You won't see pair trawling often – the practice is banned in UK waters – but continental fishing boats really do show this flag even though you might feel their lights sometimes leave much to be desired.

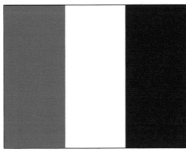

Code Flag T looks like the French ensign with the colours reversed

11   'ELLO, 'ELLO, 'ELLO!

Cruising in foreign waters, you never know when you'll be boarded by the authorities. They may leave you alone for years, then suddenly, one day, there they are! It doesn't pay to be complacent about carrying documentation. Ship's registration papers (SSR document is fine), evidence of VAT payment, skipper's licence (or at least an ICC certificate), passports, VHF certificate of competence and insurance certificate are minimum requirements in many countries. If you don't have them handy, you may be in for a rough ride.

Be prepared for a visit from the authorities

12   UPWIND OR DOWNWIND?

A summer's cruise that's planned too tightly can lead to wretchedness and mutiny. Neptune, after all, does not send his winds to serve our little purposes, and if we are set on what turns out to be a long beat at the outset, it doesn't make for happiness. On a day sail when you know the wind will not change, it makes sense to start out upwind and come home on a reach, on the 'nasty things first, nice things later' principle known to every well-brought-up baby. On a longer trip, you might put to sea upwind and arrive tired, only to see the breeze clock the following week and stuff you at home time too. Begin downwind and you've secured at least 50% joy. You've probably an even chance on your homeward passage too. At worst, you'll score 50-50, but the odds are in your favour. Ask any gambler . . .

Going to windward on day one may not make for a good start!

13 GOING DOWN WITH THE TIDE

If you keep the company of old-fashioned longshoremen and you're having tea in their shed near High Water when it's blowing like stink, one of them is bound to say, "Don't worry, lads. The wind'll go down with the tide." I expect readers well versed in science will thumb their noses at this little chunk of lore, but hold fast! There may not be a shred of truth in the idea 15 miles offshore, but in a river or on a beach flanked by shoals, more and more natural shelter appears as the sea level falls. The waves ease back, even the wind seems diminished with the water 20 ft lower down and the overall impression is undeniable. If you don't believe me, try rowing across your local river in Force 9 at High Water, then at the bottom of the tide. The old boys were right all along.

It looks fierce now, but at Low Water many more rocks will uncover to kill the seas

14 COLREG MNEMONICS

It's not easy to remember the details of the Colregs when you aren't at sea every day but in practice sometimes there isn't time to look up an obscure one. Mnemonics can help you recall them. Here's an example:

Question: Which side do you pass a dredger – ball daymarks, or diamonds?

Answer: Great balls of fire! Fire is red, so diamonds must be green. I'll go with green for safety's sake.

You can probably think up more.

Pass the dredger on the 'diamond side'

15   LIGHTEN OUR DARKNESS

Sailing into or leaving a strange harbour at night is never fun, but if you've no choice a little moonlight can make a big difference. If you can time your movements for a couple of hours or more after moonrise that's a real bonus, especially if the moon is more than half full. A decent almanac like *Reeds* will dish up the information, but it's a whole lot easier on a chart-plotter. This little electric brain will work out the exact time for where you actually are. The illustrated Garmin even tells you whether the moon is waxing, waning, full or not visible at all, and if you're a proper sailor who's interested in lowering the colours at sunset, it'll put you straight about that as well.

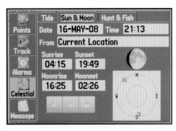

This Garmin plotter tells you the current phase of the moon

16   LEFTOVER SEAS

The chances are that, some time each season, half of us will find ourselves holed up in some faraway port while the usual mid-holiday gale blows itself out. It's tempting to stick one's nose past the mole as soon as the wind drops to Force 4, but if the heavy stuff has had an onshore component there will be a nasty sea to contend with. Typically, we could find ourselves in a falling breeze 'going up and down in the same hole' for anything up to 24 hours. The answer, of course, is to select a bolt-hole with a good pub, a nice beach, a multiplex cinema or a casino with distracted croupiers. That is real passage planning . . .

Think twice before sailing in a nasty slop left over from a gale

17   SAIL ON THE MOON TIDE

If you sail in central southern England, you'll find High Water Springs equate to midnight and midday. Down in the West Country they fall around 0600 and 1800, on the Thames they usually arrive in time for a latish lunch, and so on. Neaps clearly come six hours adrift. We all know that tides follow the moon and that the top of Springs will be a day or two after full moon or at new moon. Once you have established when your local tides generally fall, you've only to look at the moon sailing through the clouds to predict what time tomorrow's ebb will start running away, which is exactly how it was done before people had tide tables.

Use the moon to predict the tides

18   OVER THE WAVES

Making landfall in the dark, it's more than likely that you'll be looking out hard to identify lights. There could well be a sea running that's higher than your eye level as you sit at the helm. Height of eye sitting down may be as little as 4 ft in a small yacht, or 8 ft in a big one with a centre cockpit. In either case, the extra 6 ft gained by standing up at the mast makes a huge difference. What appears to be a buoy occasionally blinking might turn into an occulting lighthouse if you're high enough up to see the difference.

The Needles is a popular cross-Channel landfall – get up by the mast to spot the difference between flashing buoys and the occulting lighthouse

19   CHECKING FOR DRAG

By far the best method of observing whether or not an anchor is dragging is to find a natural transit of two objects more or less abeam when the boat is head-up to the hook. For crispness, these want to be reasonably close. You can even use another boat that looks good, so long as she doesn't join you up the beach when all goes pear-shaped. A compass being used to see if a bearing alters is a blunt instrument by comparison, only useful when no transit offers itself. Even at night, two lights, or one light in line with a silhouette on the skyline, can usually be found. The GPS receiver promising to advise optimistic skippers of a dragging hook is only of interest in dense fog.

Trust a transit when anchoring

20   PASSING IN THE NIGHT

In the daytime, giving way to a ship at sea can simply be a matter of a minor course alteration to clear his stern. Generally, 20° or 30° is more than enough. At night, it's a different story, because all he can see of you is your lights. You may be making a good radar target, but it's safest to assume you are not. For the bridge watch to know you are giving way, you must turn far enough to show him a light of a different colour. This can be inconvenient, but it's reassuring to know he's in no doubt about your intentions.

Best assume that all he's seen of you is your lights

NAVIGATION

21 THE DESTINATION

When using a chart-plotter, the destination waypoint is well worth entering, even if you don't bother with any others. It enables you to see at a glance how long you have to go, whether the destination's bearing is matching up with your passage plan, how far it is, how your VMG (speed made good towards it) compares with boat speed and ground speed and, best of all, whether you'll be in before closing time – also known as 'Estimated Time of Arrival'!

Enter a destination waypoint – it'll help you see how long you've got to go

22 KEEP A TRACK

Using a chart-plotter without activating the 'projected track' feature is like eating chips without salt and vinegar. 'Projected track' creates a line, emanating from the image of the boat, which shows where she will be in a given time, always assuming speed, current etc. remain constant. While this is never exactly true, the feature can still be of enormous value. If you can't find how to do it, either read the manual or spend half an hour scrolling the menus. It's in there somewhere!

Turn on a plotter's 'projected track' feature to see where you're heading at a glance

23   EXPLORE THAT PLOTTER

The first thing some people do when they buy a new piece of equipment is study the manual. Others fall back on the old maxim of not reading the instructions until all else has failed. Many of today's electronic chart-plotters will deliver a full breakdown of the tidal height for numerous points on the charts they incorporate, including secondary ports. What bliss that is, but it only works for navigators who've taken the trouble to discover which buttons to press. A straw poll shows that a surprising number never bother to find out. Now visit tip 41 for the full story.

Are you making the most of your chart-plotter?

24   CHECK IF IN DOUBT

If you're in doubt about the identity of a land or seamark, the easiest way to make sure of it is to plot a GPS fix on the chart and see what the bearing of the object ought to be from there. Next, nip up on deck with the hand-bearing compass and make sure the object bears as it should – always allowing for the distance run between the fix and when you finally settle on a bearing. If there is a serious discrepancy, reach for the binoculars and look again.

It's an east cardinal, but which one? A hand-bearing compass can help you be sure

25 RADAR WATCH IN THE REAL WORLD

To be fully effective, a radar operator should be watching developments almost constantly. In a small yacht, where perhaps only the skipper is qualified to interpret the screen, this may be unrealistic. Obviously, another lookout must be detailed if traffic is heavy in poor visibility, but in quieter waters when you are the sole watchkeeper, it can be hard to decide how long to spend checking the radar screen for other vessels.

One answer is to have the screen sited so as to be visible from the cockpit, then view it with the range rings switched off and the range itself set to six miles. The screen is left clear and blank, making any new blip stand out. Once a target is established, you can set up the rings, hit the Electronic Bearing Line (EBL) and Variable Range Marker (VRM), then get back to the real world on deck while watching it make its move.

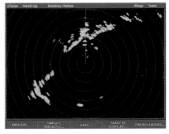

Switch the range to six miles and lose the rings for a clearer radar view

26 FOLLOW YOUR TRANSITS

This boat looks as though she ought to have smacked the buoy good and hard, but the tide has carried her clear. Try reading the current running off the buoy. As she approached it, her skipper would have seen the buoy sliding sideways along that wooded shoreline behind it and known that, even if he was pointing straight at it, he could no more hit it than fly to the moon. The transits were moving, so he was safe.

By reading the current running off a buoy and using transits, you can pinch in close

27   TIDAL OBSERVATIONS

Sailors in the central Solent, UK, can always tell the direction of the tide at Calshot by noting how the lightfloat is lying. The authorities gave this vessel an anchor ball when they towed away the old lightship many years ago. The ball is on the side of the float nearest to its mooring, so its 'up-tide' position is as clear an indicator as the bows of the anchored lightship once were.

Particularly useful around the turn of the tide, observations of this type can be made anywhere that the lie of a vessel can be observed. In some locations, buoys are actually sited on small boats. Reading these is a piece of cake. Elsewhere, only a distant anchored ship may help.

Calshot's lightfloat is an indicator of tide direction

28   NATURAL TIDE GAUGES

This chap is dropping down to the sea to cross a bar, but he doesn't need to consult his secondary port tidal height calculation to be sure of enough water. He's already observed on a previous day that he has enough clearance to proceed if the shoal offshore of him is almost awash. Of course, the shingle might change its characteristics in the next big gale. So, for that matter, may the bar itself. For the time being, however, he knows beyond doubt that he is safe.

Shoal

Mk 1 eyeball beats science again!

29 HOW FAR FROM SHORE ARE YOU ANCHORED?

Any old hand knows that an anchored boat looks tighter in to the rocks from her deck than she ever does from the shore. A useful reassurance if you have radar is to set the electronic range ring to touch the nearest rocks and see how close they really are. In this case, the skipper has set the ring to the same diameter as the scope of cable he has laid. As a further refinement, he has estimated the probable position of his anchor and placed the cursor on it to delineate his swinging room requirement.

The electronic chart reproduction of the same situation backs up the radar image by delivering data from an independent source. A sound plan, because the rocks just might be a poor radar target.

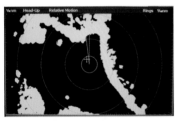 

Note that the chart is set at north-up, while the radar is head-up. The arrow on the chart represents only the most recent swing of the boat and has nothing to do with her present aspect. The boat is actually head-up into the cove south of her

30 USING THE PLOTTER

Running a plotter isn't all that hard. Even if some of your crew aren't official navigators, teach them to use the plotter as a common-sense visual tool. Show them how to pan and zoom and make sure they understand the scale of things. Then, when you're off watch, they'll have another tool to help orientate themselves and interpret what they're seeing.

Teach your crew how to use the plotter

31 DATUM SHIFT – THE LURKING BANDIT OF THE PLOTTER

Here's a photo taken in June 2006 of a yacht on a plotter screen. She appears to be parked in the local supermarket; she is actually secure alongside the wall at the eastern end of the dock. The distance to the supermarket was something over 200 m. Nothing was wrong with the plotter's configuration – the fault lay in a rift between the GPS lat long data and the electronic chart itself. In other words, a classic datum shift. When you think what could have happened to the yacht had her skipper relied on total plotter accuracy, entering this harbour in fog, there's no need to say more.

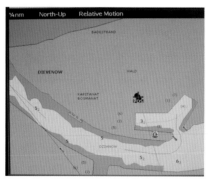

The chart-plotter shows this yacht parked ashore, when she's actually alongside the quay

32 PILOTING WITH RADAR

When it comes to confirming distance off a solid object, such as a cliff, the most accurate tool on board a fully equipped skipper is radar. A good example is rounding Portland Bill, keeping a cable or two offshore to stay in the deep water, but safe inside the boiling tide race to seaward. It takes nerve to stay so close, but there's no transit, so radar it is – if you have it! Choose the most appropriate range, hit the button to activate the variable range marker (VRM) and set the circle to the chosen distance off. Double-check that you haven't committed a nonsense, then go ahead, keeping the VRM just touching the echo of the cliff. Don't forget to watch the echo sounder for that vital cross-check, and remember that the final arbiter is still your own eyes. They'll soon tell you if you've made a major error.

Use radar to maintain a constant offing

33 IDENTIFYING MARKS

You've spotted this buoy through the binoculars, but there are others not too far away. It's critical that you have the right one, so how do you make sure? The easy answer is to steer across to the left of the picture so that the buoy comes into transit with the unambiguous headland, then note its compass bearing. Now read the bearing of the transit off the chart. If it doesn't coincide with your observation, either the buoy is off-station or it's the wrong one. Don't expect split-degree accuracy here. Buoys are not fixed objects, but for these purposes, they're usually close enough to call.

How do you make sure this is the right buoy?

34 DATUMS FOR GPS

The datum of a chart is found in amongst the title data. Once you know what is – for example, 'Ordnance Survey of Great Britain (OSGB) 1936' – you have two choices if you intend to plot onto it. Ideally, reset your GPS receiver (search the set-up menus) to this datum. If you can't do that, use the 'Satellite Derived Positions' information to adjust your GPS plot, but only when super-accuracy really matters. Most of the time, when you are out at sea, such issues are of academic interest only, but when you're looking for a buoy in dense fog, they can make all the difference.

Know the datum of your chart, and synch your GPS

35 A QUICK FIX

If your GPS goes down and you don't fancy a major plotting bonanza to fix your position, look for an identifiable object ahead or astern (somewhat off your course if need be – Dungeness light in this example). Steer to bring it right onto the bow or dead aft. The steering compass is now reading the bearing or its reciprocal, and it's an instant line of position. Hold that heading, and wait until a second charted feature (Rye Fairway) comes abeam. The best way of knowing this accurately is to wait until it lines up with the 'gun sight' of the mainsheet traveller, the aft cockpit coaming or the aft face of the coachroof. Because the buoy is now at 90° from your heading, you don't need to take its bearing.

Plotting this perfect 'cut' is a pushover. Set your chart protractor to the ship's heading, with Dungeness (A) ahead or astern, then lay it across the chart in such a way that the square edge falls on the buoy (B). The corner of the plotter is your fix (C). Pop your cross on the chart, enter it in the logbook, and hurry back to the action.

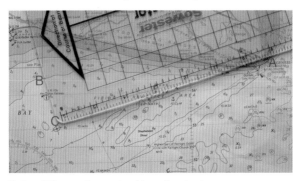

If your GPS goes down, plot this perfect 'cut'

36 ESTIMATED POSITIONS

If you are obliged to plot a traditional estimated position at more than one hour from your departure point, don't try to do it hour by hour. Instead, plot the dead reckoning position for the whole leg from course steered and distance run, then plot the tides on the end in one-hour chunks.

37 KEEP CLEAR

If you're an habitué of the North Sea you'll be aware of the fact that the small rings charted around gas and oil platforms mean you must keep at least 500 m clear. If you're just passing through, you might have missed the note on the chart, so look out for the pecked circle. At night, most of these platforms and associated structures flash out Morse code 'Uniform'. In old money, this means "You are standing into danger"!

Observe the pecked circle on the chart and keep clear of those oil and gas platforms

38 STEERING BY EYE

Where an entrance you fancy is encumbered by shoals extending from one or both sides, it's surprising how accurately you can judge them with nothing more than 'Mk 1 eyeball'.

Approaching square-on, it's easy to place an imaginary mark halfway across. Now divide each half into two and you've got pretty reasonable quarters. Chopping the gap into three parts can also be achieved with surprising accuracy. Check the chart and, so long as things aren't too tight, you may well find that one of these imaginary lines will lead safely in, or clear a rock shelf. If in doubt, though, give it a miss.

This entrance looks simple, but there's a submerged rock a third of the way across

39 A LIFELINE IN THE FOG

When we move into the foggiest months of the year we are so much safer than we used to be, thanks to GPS. However, nobody but a madman would navigate in fog on the assured assumption that the instrument can't fail.

In the days of dead reckoning, any buoy looming up was logged for time and distance before the pilot drew another breath. A free fix and a fresh departure! When manna descended from Heaven to the starving Israelites it was not more gratefully received. Even with a GPS chart-plotter to reassure us, failing to log a buoy in bad visibility might prove a costly mistake. Imagine going below to discover an empty screen, 20 minutes after ignoring a buoy with a name on it!

Don't forget to record the name of any buoys you see when sailing in fog – you never know when the chart-plotter might fail!

40 CHANGING CHARTS

We'd all like to keep our charts corrected as per the book, but for some of us it isn't always possible. Perhaps we're too busy making ends meet, maybe our folio is too huge to contemplate the number of *Notices to Mariners* we'd need, or maybe we're just bone idle. Whatever our excuse, and however we may mutter about 'the rocks not moving', sometimes we really need to be certain where the buoys and lights are. Even if our charts are as old as this one, however, all is not lost. *Reed's Almanac* carries lists of all navigation marks for each sea area with positions and characteristics. They're updated to the most recent publication. Not perfect, but a lot better than most people's charts!

Consult the almanac if you want to double-check the position of navigation marks

41 TAKE DEPTH PREDICTIONS WITH A PINCH OF SALT

These days, secondary port tidal heights don't hold the terrors they used to – not if you've a plotter, that is. Here's a readout from a PC unit. Most hardware plotters offer the same service, if you know where to find it, and it means an end to struggling with interpolation and graphs.

There's only one problem. Your plotter's figure may well be different to the one being delivered by another manufacturer's kit on the yacht 50 yards away. Most of the time, these readouts are fairly useful, but when you've cut things fine and need to know the tide to decimals of a metre, perhaps it's time to lick your pencil, get out the tables and hit the graph after all. Even then, your best-calculated result remains a prediction. Only the fishes know how deep it really is.

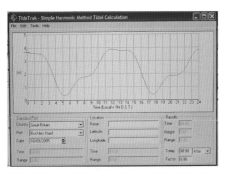

Digital tide predictions may look authoritative, but don't trust them completely

42 SPELL IT OUT TO STAY ON COURSE

This boat is heading at 'three-two-five'. If the navigator asks the helm to steer 'three-twenty-five' he'll get what he wants just the same. But if the course had been 315 ('three-one-five') and he'd said 'three-fifteen', he could have been misheard on a windy night. The boat would have gone barrelling off on 'three-fifty', and Lord knows where she'd have ended up. Three single-digit figures, including an 'oh' where appropriate (or a 'zero' if you prefer), leave no room for doubt.

Three single-digit figures leave no room for doubt

43   WAYPOINTS FOR DANGER

We're all used to placing waypoints in safe places, but sometimes the best technique for avoiding an unmarked isolated danger is to pop a waypoint right on top of it. It's especially useful when you're using a paper chart and you don't actually mind which side you pass the problem. As the waypoint approaches, all you need do is make sure its bearing is altering, just as you would with a visual object. So long as it's on the move, you can't hit it. Plot the waypoint like this one and you'll be able to see what you're missing!

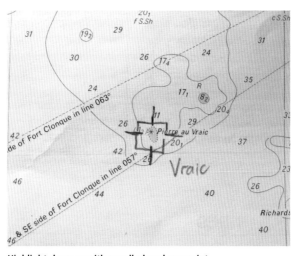

Highlight dangers with a well-placed waypoint

44   COMPENSATING FOR LEEWAY

Unless you're a professor of mathematics who can think in pure numbers, the easiest way to plot a course compensating for leeway is visually. Whack in the course you really want, then literally sketch the wind direction on the chart. It's obvious now which way to steer 'up' so as to have the boat slide along the desired track. Plot a small line to indicate this, and that's the course to hand up to the helm. As to how many degrees to apply, that's another story. If in doubt, go for 7°...

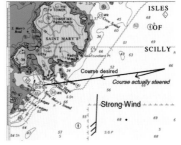

To allow for leeway, make a simple visual plot

45   OVERTAKEN BY TIME

"Spot the entrance by looking just east of the Martello Tower," warbles the pilot book. The trouble is, any pilot is only as good as its compiler's most recent visit. In a place with massive development going on continually, it's only reasonable to expect a certain amount of misinformation from a book that isn't updated annually. Don't be too hard on the writer. The advice was sound when he delivered it and if he's on the ball he'll get it right next time around. In the meantime, when you see edifices like these going up to dwarf the landmarks of the ages, the best bet is a swift GPS waypoint near the harbour entrance!

New housing can obscure landmarks

46   WILL SHE, WON'T SHE?

Bridge clearances on Admiralty charts are given at 'HAT' (Highest Astronomical Tide) – you're unlikely to find any less air draught. All very well, until your calculations suggest there's only a metre or two above the Windex. Then, as you approach the span, it all starts to look frightfully tight. Obviously, one answer is to proceed as slowly as possible. A better plan is to station 'a boy of little consequence' at the masthead. When there's a strong fair tide and no volunteers for the climb, try stemming the stream and letting it carry you through astern over the ground. You'll have total control over your speed and can ram the throttle hard down to escape unscathed if you scrape the ironwork with your spar.

Approaching a bridge can be heart-stopping

47 THE INSIDE PASSAGE THAT ISN'T THERE

Pilot books and local sailors love to recommend their favourite inside passages where a terrible tide race is raging just a quarter-mile offshore. Many inshore passages are highly reliable, some less so, and it pays to prepare for the worst. Some passages are very narrow indeed and it doesn't take much to transform what should be a millpond into wall-to-wall breakers. The best advice is, if conditions seem OK, go for it, but look out ahead for that white water. Keep the harnesses handy, and be ready to batten down.

St Alban's: an inshore passage that can turn unexpectedly rough on the wrong day

48 INSTANT POSITION LINES

When you're piloting close inshore, things can happen too fast for you to take and plot magnetic position lines. Here's how to check bearings without the hand-bearing compass.

- Object abeam: if an object can be sighted along the mainsheet traveller, or across the companionway, you're home and dry. Read the steering compass, then add or subtract 90°.
- Object ahead or astern: again, you can read the steering compass almost without preparation or thinking. If the object is within 30° of bow or stern, jink off-course to bring it momentarily ahead or astern. It's so much easier than using the hand-bearing compass.

For a bearing on the lighthouse, just steer towards it and read the main compass

49 TIME THOSE LIGHTS

What, precisely, does 'Fl (3) 15s' mean to the practical navigator? Obviously, it's a light flashing in a group of three at 15-second intervals. But when do you start counting?

The answer is, begin as soon as you see the first flash and carry on numbering up the seconds until the same flash comes around again. Whether a light flashes or occults, the time period is the whole cycle, not just the period of darkness.

It pays to train yourself to count seconds accurately. Try the old standby: 'a thousand and one, a thousand and two …' It works like a charm up to 20 seconds.

Train yourself to count the seconds accurately

50 A PATH THROUGH THE ROCKS

Even a chart-plotter can sometimes be wrong. Threading your way through a well-trodden but tiny pass in the rocks, the smallest datum shift can put you in dire danger. The men who erected transit markers like this one centuries ago knew that if they got it wrong, they might well be hung in the town square, which concen-

trated their minds on getting it dead right. A transit doesn't purport to tell the whole story, but when you're threading through reefs, all you need is to know you won't hit them. The transit cuts right to the chase.

In any case, it's a lot easier to look at two objects lined up ahead of you than to respond to a virtual-reality screen – especially with a surge running.

One of the arts of modern naviga-tion is knowing when to revert to the ancient ways.

Transits are immune from datum errors!

51   SERIOUS CORNERS

Many headlands deliver an hour's 'free tide' on an inshore eddy just before the main turn, but when it comes to serious corners such as Land's End, Dover Strait or the Chenal du Four, a veritable gravy train may be on offer from the stream. Here's a classic example:

A 40-footer with a southerly wind can leave the marina at Brest 2 1/2 hours before Low Water and sail the 15 miles to Pointe de St Mathieu on the last of the ebb. Here, she picks up the first of the north-going tide to sweep her up the 20 miles of the Chenal du Four just in time to grab the early east-going eddy inshore at Portsall.

If she presses on with a big tide under her, she can then carry the main flood for almost seven hours. This gets her nearly to Trébeurden, another 50 miles on, with an hour to spare before the sill flops shut. What a day!

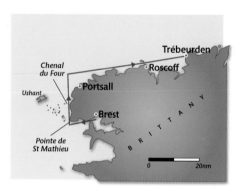

You can carry 14 hours of fair tide from Brest!

52   OVER THE FALLS

Just because the chart has no overfalls symbol in a specific area off a headland, it doesn't mean there won't be any. If it's been blowing hard (or still is) and the tide is rattling round to weather, assume the worst and batten well down. You might get a pleasant surprise but if you receive a thorough dusting instead, at least you'll be ready for it!

Nearly all headlands can produce overfalls

53 DAMN DECIMALS

Here's a typical GPS readout of a lat/long position, giving three decimal places. To put this in perspective, two decimal places give accuracy to 20 yards. The third is purporting to pinpoint the boat's location to within the span of our outstretched arms – a fathom.

It's hard to imagine anything other than the most accurate harbour chart being drawn to anywhere near this degree of precision, never mind any datum issues. More often than not, then, for the practical purposes of the cruising sailor, the last number is a waste of time.

On most occasions, we need only read the first 'point' of a mile. On a passage chart, the pencil line thickness may be that in itself. Wrestling with more decimal places than we need to winds up stress and encourages number-crunching errors. There's a time and place for everything.

Navigator	
Lat	50 17.898N
Lng	1 03.381W
	●●
COG	182.6
SOG	5.4 30 Err. (m)
ROT	0
Hd T	180.0 D 47.0 m
UTC	12:05:03 (12:05)

Decimal points – a waste of time?

54 HIDDEN DANGERS

Yachtsmen are optimistic souls, but when it comes to guessing what's beneath the water it's best to err on the side of caution. At High Water, all you can see of Black Rock at the mouth of the River Fal is the top half of the mark, and the temptation is to think that the obstruction lies directly beneath. This shot shows how far the rocky ledges extend. If in doubt, stay well out.

Don't be fooled into thinking the obstruction lies directly beneath a mark. It often doesn't ...

55   COG, SOG AND THE LOG

The need to maintain regular logbook entries has not been compromised by either GPS or the chart-plotter. Any log carries columns for 'log reading' and 'course steered'. Race boats might add 'speed through the water'. These are still important, but two extra columns make sense today: COG ('course over ground', or 'track') and SOG ('speed over ground') can be read off the GPS and entered in seconds.

The logbook provides data to work up an estimated position. If your GPS packs up, the log may conk out as well, but it's unlikely we'll lose track of time, which has always linked speed to distance. If COG and SOG have remained reasonably steady, they offer an excellent path to finding a new position.

On this unit, COG is 'track' and SOG is 'speed'

56   CHECK THE WAYPOINT

If you're navigating with GPS and a paper chart, the easiest way to check each waypoint is first to punch them into the GPS on your home mooring using lat/long coordinates lifted from the chart. Next, activate each one in turn and note its range and bearing from your present position. You know where you are right now, because you're at home. Use your dividers and protractor to see if the reality on the chart stacks up with numbers on the screen. If there's a discrepancy, check those lat/long figures again!

Checking a waypoint from your mooring. Do the range and bearing stack up with the actual position of the waypoint on the chart?

57 THE DOUBLE TRANSIT

Every skipper knows about lining up two objects 'in transit' to keep the boat on a straight track in a cross-tide. What's less obvious is monitoring both sides of a gap, such as this entrance at Honfleur in the Seine Estuary. Cross-tides run very hard here, so it's important to hit the entrance around dead-centre, but there's no leading line to follow. The answer is to watch both pier heads and make sure that the background is 'opening' from both of them at once. If one starts revealing less behind it while the other shows more, you're on the slippery sideways slope.

Watch both pier heads if you don't have a transit

58 DEPTH SUMS MADE EASY

The calculation to avoid involuntary drying out when anchoring on a falling tide is a lot easier than many imagine. Forget trying to interpolate between tiny soundings on the chart to guess the depth where you are. Just fill out the tidal height curve (or use the one on the chart-plotter), see what the height of tide is now and note what it will be at Low Water. The difference is how much the tide will fall.

It only remains to add this figure to the depth you want to be lying in at the bottom of the tide, sound in until you find it, and drop the hook.

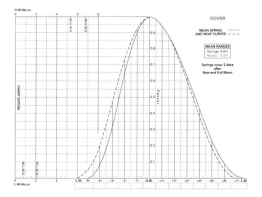

The almanac's tidal height curves makes depth sums easy

59 PAYING THE RATES

If you haven't studied for a Yachtmaster theory course for a while, you've probably forgotten about the 'computation of rates' table that sits quietly minding its own business at the front of an *Admiralty Tidal Stream Atlas*. You won't find one in your almanac. The table's sole purpose is to interpolate between the spring and neap figures for any tidal arrow inside the book, and it is a lot easier to use than it looks. All you do is make a pencil mark on the 'neap' dotted line for the neap tidal speed, and another one on the spring line for the spring velocity. On this example, they are 1.0 knot and 2.1 knots. Draw a straight line joining the dots. Now take a peep in the tide tables to discover the range of tide for the day (the difference between High and Low Water). Enter the table on the left-hand side with this value and trundle across to the line you've drawn. Now go up to the rate axis and read it off. If the range here were 4.8 m, the rate would be 1.6 knots.

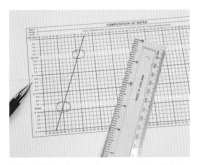

This table's a lot easier to use than it looks

60 CAN'T SEE IT FOR LOOKING AT IT

Can't find the buoy or pier head you're looking for from seawards? Check the chart for a really conspicuous object on the shore that you can bring directly behind it. Note the bearing of the transit formed by the two objects and steer to a position where the conspicuous one is on that bearing. The one you're hunting will be directly in front of it.

You can't miss the church, but the beacon would be hard to spot without it

61 STANDARD PRESSURE

The predicted tide height can vary by a foot or more depending on atmospheric pressure. Wind and other local factors are important, too, but less easy to second-guess unless you know your area.

All tidal height predictions assume 'standard pressure' on the barometer. You can take this to be 1,013 millibars (mb). If the pressure rises 30 mb above this, the extra 'weight' of air will sit on the tide and depress it by about 1 ft, or 0.3 m. At 30 mb below 1,013 mb, the tide will rise 0.3 m higher than predicted. That's 0.6 m between 983 mb and 1,043 mb. In-between is pro rata and, remember, any variation affects the whole tide – High Water, Low Water and all levels in between.

You've worked out the tide, but how sure can you be of the prediction?

62 MAN IS NOT LOST

With GPS so reliable, it's easy to become complacent in fog. Looking for Chichester Bar beacon? Just bung in a waypoint and hit 'Go To'. But what if the beacon was moved last year and the chart on the charter boat you're on does not show its new position? Updating a modest folio of charts is easy these days. No more waiting for the *Notices to Mariners* to arrive, then ploughing through pages of stuff about Singapore. Just go to www.nmwebsearch.com click on the sort of charts you're using and select the chart you want updating. No more blundering in the dark!

Updating charts has never been easier

63   ONE IN A HUNDRED

Because the nautical mile is about 2,000 yards in length, it is also more or less 6,000 ft. Conveniently, there are 60 minutes in one hour, which means that, in one minute, a boat travelling at one knot will have moved ahead by 100 ft. This gets better, because at any speed, you only have to multiply the number of knots by 100 and that's the distance you cover in a minute. If you lose a crew member overboard and hit the MOB button on the GPS, the casualty will be drifting away from the fix at 100 ft multiplied by the tidal stream in knots every minute. If you haven't got him back in six minutes with the tide given as two knots, he's 1,200 ft – almost a quarter of a mile – from the fix already.

You've hit the MOB button, but will he stay put?

64   ONE FINAL WAYPOINT

On a passage of some length – South Coast to Cherbourg, for example – it's tempting to make the final waypoint at the outer harbour entrance. After dark, however, shore lighting can make spotting the lights of the inner harbour and the associated buoys difficult, especially for first-timers who haven't seen the place in daylight. Add a touch of mist or real fog, and you're lost in no time. The answer is to plot an extra waypoint or two at the planning stage. When you arrive, beware of potential collisions with other meandering mariners.

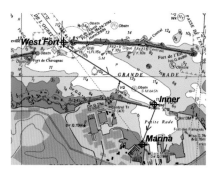

Plot extra waypoints for night-time arrivals

65 OVERFALLS AND THE PASSAGE PLAN

Planning a passage on an electronic vector chart, it's vital to zoom well in at any headlands or other pinch points. The nature of the beast is that vital details are often 'layered out' by the processor at planning scales. In these images, the zoomed-out chart fails to show the nasty tide rips off the headland that are clearly visible when the chart is examined more closely. The other answer is, of course, to plan on a paper chart or its raster-scan equivalent. With these, what you see is what you get, so long as you've chosen the right scale to start with.

Zoom well in or you'll miss crucial information

66 LEEWAY – THE EASY WAY

Here's an easy system for making sure you apply leeway correctly on a course to steer. First, construct your one-hour plot; next, sketch the wind on the chart. As soon as you can see which way it's blowing you, it's obvious how to adjust the course to compensate. Draw in a short line to show what you are going to do, then hand this modified course up to the helmsman.

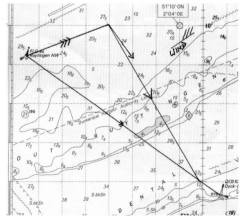

Draw the wind on the chart to make leeway calculations clearer

67 SINGLE POSITION LINES AND GPS

It's natural to think of GPS in terms of a full fixing system or a means of tracking to waypoints, but waypoints take time and effort to input and it isn't always necessary to go to the trouble of plotting a fix. Often, a single lat or long coordinate is all that's needed. This skipper is sailing along a strange coast looking for a harbour entrance in poor visibility. The tide is sluicing along and he has plenty else to think about. In fact, all he needs to do is note the longitude of the entrance. When he's on it, it must bear due south.

It's surprising how many other uses can be found for a single position line which, when you think about it, is all a latitude or a longitude really is.

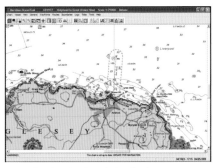

Note the longitude of the harbour entrance. When you're on it, head due south

68 ELECTRONIC BEACONS

Here is a safe line defined on the chart by a distant transit that's notoriously difficult to spot. To overcome the problem, plot a waypoint on it. Coming in from the north, you're safe on the blue line but it's OK to stray as far east as the black line. So long as the waypoint's bearing stays between the lines, you're as safe as if you had a bearing on a visible beacon – in fact, you're safer, because instead of relying on a wavering compass bearing, the bearing of the electronic beacon pops up as a solid and accurate number on the GoTo screen. However, don't forget to ensure that the chart and the unit are working to the same datum.

Plot a waypoint to firm up a transit that's hard to see

69 KEEP 'EM HANDY

A useful way to encourage the hands to wear harness tethers on deck is to make it easy. Instead of hanging them around your neck when they may not be wanted, try keeping them hitched either side of the cockpit, with one end clipped to the jackstay ready for action, the other on the guardrail. Anyone already going forward wearing a deflated lifejacket now has two choices. Either clamber over the thing (inconvenient) or grab it and clip it to the lifejacket ring (easy as falling over the side!).

Clip on and stay aboard

70 SALVAGE!

Always discuss the deal before you accept a tow. If you've run out of fuel on a calm evening, a friendly fisherman might pull you in for a bottle of scotch, but if your boat is in undisputed danger and you accept a tow willy-nilly, you may be rendering your insurers at risk of a salvage claim. Make certain the arrangements are understood by both parties. If the circumstances allow, and you are in any doubt, contact your insurers. It could save you more than any other call you make.

Salvage fees can be costly, so make sure both parties are agreed on the terms

71 POT NIGHTMARE

In these days of radar and pin-point chart-plotters, it's becoming ever more tempting to steer close in around headlands in calm weather after dark, especially if you're cheating a foul tide. The trouble is, fishermen love laying their crab pots well inshore over those nice juicy rock bottoms. The pots aren't charted and they generally don't show up well on radar. If the current's strong enough you might even miss them in daylight because they've literally been towed under.

Some areas are worse than others, but spending the night moored by the propeller as the tide whooshes under your stern remains one of a skipper's worst nightmares.

Watch out for pots around headlands

72 CARRY A MASK

All yachts should carry a simple mask and snorkel for that evil day when the propeller gets wrapped up. Flippers are good, too, but not essential.

Cutting the shaft free of fishing tackle, mooring ropes or even the skipper's underwear is not difficult for a swimmer armed with a serrated blade such as a good bread knife or a hacksaw. But you must be able to see what you're doing. A few quid spent in a seaside store could save a lifeboat call-out.

A mask is a sensible piece of safety kit

73 'READY ABOUT!' BUT 'STAND BY TO GYBE!'

These are the traditional orders. 'Ready about' means 'sort your-selves out for a tack' and 'stand by to gybe' means 'get that mainsheet hove in and keep your heads down!'

When 'ready about' is called, many skippers won't tack until the crew have responded that they've prepared their sheets and winches.

If a skipper says, 'ready to gybe' and the hands only hear the word 'ready' in heavy weather, it could lead to discord and the wrong result. 'Stand by to gybe' is unambiguous. It also needs no response because, even on a pitch black night, the person giving the order will have a pretty good idea when the sheet has been pulled in. Keep the two orders sepa-rate and there'll never be a misunderstanding.

The use of correct orders ensures clear communication on board

74 WHIPLASH

When you're releasing a snap shackle under load, on a cruising chute perhaps, keep your face averted and well clear of the action. Lines suddenly released from tension can turn themselves into a good facsimile of a circus ringmaster's whip!

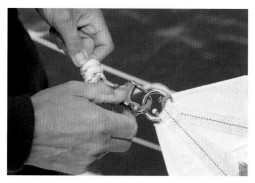

Watch out for whiplash

75 KEEP PEERING AROUND THAT CORNER

We all know that a deep-bodied genoa totally blocks off all vision on the lee bow, especially when you're close-hauled and well heeled over. The person on the helm has a sector of anything up to 60° where he or she is totally blind. Boats can creep up into this zone with amazing rapidity, especially the ones you just missed seeing last time you peeped around the leech, so detail someone off to look out, and keep them at it. It's a great job for a youngster who's been getting bored and needs responsibility!

If you sit to leeward to see beneath the genoa, you'll need the crew looking out too

76 UNSEEN DANGERS

Be aware of the possibility that renewable energy facilities at sea may give rise to two unexpected dangers. The presence of large quantities of steel, cabling and electricity may cause local magnetic anomalies that can upset a compass severely. There is also a concern that interference from such developments will cause radar users to turn down their gain control to clean up the picture. They'll still be able to see the supertankers, but the likes of us may disappear altogether. Forewarned is forearmed!

Could this wind farm render us vulnerable to collision?

77 DROP BEFORE YOU DIP

If you enjoy swimming from the boat, remember to drop the ladder before you take the plunge. It's easy to forget, and even yachts with modern bathing platforms can be tricky to board from the water. Singlehanding, you could be in real bother. If there's a strong current running, consider trailing a fender on the end of a long line and try to swim up-current of the boat. Swimming in open water with the boat floating free, don't underestimate how quickly she'll move because of windage, even in light airs.

Deploy it before you dive in!

78 BEWARE OF THE TUG

Everybody loves a tugboat, but love can turn to hate and real danger if you come too close to a big one on passage. Large, seagoing tugs have short waterlines and the heftiest engines in the galaxy. When not towing, they often cruise at high speed, dragging a disproportionate wash. At night, especially in confined waters, it's easy to be caught napping. If there's any reason to suspect that a vessel showing a single steaming light may be a tug not towing, give him a very wide berth indeed. The wash will fill a yacht's cockpit in the blink of an eye.

Large tugboats can create a monstrous wash!

BOAT-HANDLING

79 KEEP IT ON THE WINCH

Before self-tailing winches, a sheet was always cleated off after winding it in. Many of today's yachts don't have sheet cleats, leaving no choice but to rely on the self-tailing jaws. This is all very well until someone tumbles against a winch where the jaws weren't completely clamped into the ropework. The sheet is knocked out and away it goes. Nasty.

This will never happen if you flick an extra turn around the winch after you have finished winding. It can be as slack as you like, because its purpose is merely to guard against the unforeseen. If Clumsy Cuthbert catches his boot in it and unwinds it, the only result will be the loss of a turn that is doing nothing anyway.

Throw on an extra turn after you've finished winding

80 THE CRUEL SEA

There's a sea that's running just outside this harbour wall while inside it's lovely and calm. This yacht has come outside to hoist her mainsail and right now her crew are wishing they'd slowed down in the flat water and done the job there. It's even more true when the sail has to be lowered and stowed. Even if things are a bit tight inside, careful planning and good use of available space can often save wrestling with armfuls of canvas when the boat is rolling her rails under. It's safer, too.

Hoist sails in harbour if there's a sea running

81 MAINSAIL ONLY

All sorts of boat-handling manoeuvres under sail are more easily executed under mainsail only. Often, they involve sailing close-hauled, which is where problems can arise. A close-hauled headsail 'bends' the wind around the back of the mainsail, which

means the main must be sheeted in very hard to stop it back-winding – often almost to the yacht's centre-line. This is fine so long as it's working in conjunction with the genoa. If it is sheeted in tightly without a sail forward of it, the magic stops working and the power is virtually all sideways. Maximum leeway, minimum drive. Without the curved air coming off the jib, the main can be eased well off, even when the boat is only 45° from the true wind. She'll point just as high, go twice as fast and, more importantly, will steer like a dream.

Ease off the sheet when sailing under mainsail alone

82 FACE UP TO HIM

If you want to be heard from the other end of the boat, turn and face the folks you're talking to. It's amazing how the breeze carries your voice away if you don't.

If the wind is in your face as you try and communicate, then you'll need to shout or contrive some hand signals that work for you and your crew.

Face the person you are talking to

83 GET YOUR WEIGHT INTO IT

Winding a winch when it's tough going, you need to get your weight right over the job, even if it means having one foot outside the cockpit. A good guide is that you would be looking straight down the handle hole if you weren't watching what you're doing, which, of course, as a good crew you will be!

Putting your weight right over the winch will make winding it in easier

84 A SWEET LEAD

Lead a loaded line onto a cleat as in picture 1 and you will always be able to ease it under perfect control by holding the necessary turns. Clap it on like picture 2 and you're very likely doomed as soon as the weight comes on. The crossing turn can jam up as easily as slipping on a wet deck.

(1)	(2)

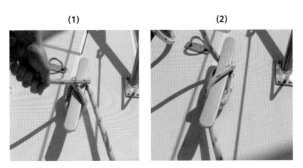

The right (1) and the wrong (2) way to lead a loaded line

85 LOOK BEHIND YOU!

When you're on watch in a following breeze, be extra vigilant regarding the wind strength. A considerable increase in force won't feel like much when you're running, and the boat may not start to complain until it's nearly too late. Reefing can then be a major drama. Keep your wits about you, and tell the skipper if you even suspect that the wind may be getting up.

Keep an eye on the wind strength when on a run

86 ADJUST YOUR CARS

A system like this makes moving the sheet car a breeze. For the full genoa, just move it fore or aft until any tell-tales at the top and bottom of the luff 'lift' at the same time when you're a few degrees above close-hauled. If the top ones 'break' first, move it forward; if the bottom ones go first, shunt it aft. When the sail is reefed you probably won't have any tell-tales, so you'll have to do it by eye alone. It will almost certainly need sliding forward. It's easy to say, "Oh, I won't bother. I'm not a racing person." But a quarter-knot is a quarter-knot, and it's 6 miles in 24 hours. A whole hour freezing at sea when you could have been snug in the pub!

Move your sheet-lead for extra boat speed

87   EASY ON THE CHAFE

Here's a neat solution for dealing with the sheets of a rolled genoa when a removable inner forestay is set up. Left to themselves, they'll chafe the blade jib. A couple of karabiners on short strops grab the bight of the genoa sheets and hold them clean out of the way. While you're up forward, lash the genoa clew with a short length of line to back up the sheets. Led downwards, they won't keep the sail rolled as reliably as they do in normal mode when the apparent wind rises to gale force.

Clip genny sheets out of the way to avoid chafe

88   DON'T BELIEVE THE HELMSMAN

Helmsmen rank among the world's most chronic liars. They're not born crooked, but fore-and-aft-rigged sailing yachts on a reach always want to screw up to windward. Broad-beamed modern craft are specialists, but even classics give their best shot to poking their noses above the course. It takes a skilled helm not to succumb to the tendency to steer a few degrees too high, even if it matters less nowadays because we have GPS and are not so reliant on estimated positions. So never mind what they tell you they've been steering. They're all at it! Watch them, and add a few degrees to weather.

All helmsmen need watching – even if they aren't on the phone!

89   REDUCE SAIL DOWNWIND – THE EASY WAY

Most of us have been taught at some time or other that we must spill wind from the mainsail before we can reef it with conventional systems. On all but the biggest yachts, this just isn't true. On passage in an increasing blow downwind with the boom preventer rigged, rounding up to reef can be downright dangerous. It's far better to running in the lessened apparent wind, hold on to the kicker and preventer, take up slack in the topping lift and ease the halyard gingerly, dragging the luff down at the same time. Heave the clew pennant down as you go, to dissuade the battens from fouling on the shrouds. Just work away at it, one bit at a time. It won't take long. The downside is that you won't be able to tie in the outer reef points, but you'll be very pleased with the seamanlike way you've handled your boat.

Try reefing downwind without rounding up

90   BOW THRUSTERS

These are a revelation on boats with shallow bows that blow around like paper bags at slow speed. If you have one, use it positively in long bursts. The mark of the beginner is to jab at it like a button on a video game console. And watch out for pickup lines being drawn into thrusters. It can happen all too easily.

Use your thruster positively, in long bursts

91   SHAPE OF THE WATER

This photograph was taken coming through Hurst Narrows in the Western Solent in moderately calm conditions. The two tidal streams (North Channel and Needles Channel) are meeting in the moving tide rip known as 'The Trap'. You can see the water is cutting up interestingly. It takes little imagination to guess what it will do in a gale of wind with the tide running to weather. Approaching an area of turbulence indicated on the chart, you can often assess how serious it really is by looking through binoculars, but don't be fooled too easily. What appears to be a bit of disturbance from a mile away can change into series of square holes in the ocean when it's too late!

Scan the sea for rough patches and steer around them

92   BE DISOBEDIENT

Judge the available berths for yourself. If the *marinero* or some self-appointed assistant on the dock starts telling you to go into one you don't like the look of, give him your straight opinion. After all, it's you who will mess it up. Some end-on berths are impossible in a big crosswind or an onshore blow. Don't go there, even if the 'experts' are shouting at you. Sort something else out, or cruise away and anchor behind a headland.

Don't let marina crew bully you into an unsuitable berth

93 DITCH EXTRA WINDAGE

Next time you're anchored and the weather is deteriorating badly, have a serious think about unnecessary windage. Lower your sprayhood – very likely, that'll save you 10 square feet at deck level. If you drop your roller genoa and bag it below, you'll be typically seven square feet to the good. Lower the boom end and lash it to the quarter, getting its windage as low as possible. Drop all bunting. Have you ever felt the pull of a flag halyard that's loaded up in a gale?

Should the anchor drag, you'll be left with engine only, but you have to ask yourself whether you could really sail out of danger in storm-force winds. Better to make sure the batteries are charged and the fuel's clean.

Windage is critical in a storm

94 CALIBRATE THE LOG

The easiest way to calibrate a log is to wait until you're between two locks somewhere – in a Dutch canal, for instance – note the speed over ground (SOG) from the GPS and set the log speed accordingly. You won't be far out. Failing a lock, you can use the same simple system if you can find some genuinely slack water as noted by the local lobster-pot buoys, but don't expect the world. Slack water isn't that reliable.

Alternatively, choose a steady current and motor at a constant speed straight into it. You can check whether you're achieving this by making sure the course over the ground (COG) lines up with the compass. Note the SOG, turn through 180° and motor down the reciprocal course at the same speed. Note the SOG again and take the average of the two. That's your boat speed. Set the log to it and you're done.

It's easiest to calibrate the log in slack water

95   OUT OF ARM'S WAY

Throttles mounted on steering pedestals can be hard to get to without reaching through the wheel. While it's tempting to take this short cut, it's advisable to reach around just in case the wheel spins unexpectedly. This is especially true when motoring astern, as the water flowing past the rudder can cause the wheel to swing with great force.

Reach around, not through the spokes

96   DOUBLING UP ON ANCHOR POWER

Anyone who usually anchors in tidal rivers could be forgiven for abandoning any ideas of setting an extra hook. It's all very well reading about swivels, rolling hitches on the bight of a cable below the water, and 'Bahamian moors', but the possibilities for any of these to lead to tangles and grief can put you right off.

It's a different story in an open roadstead, lying head to wind. There, hanging off your best bower and not liking the look of the weather, it's very simple to load the biggest spare anchor into the dinghy with a length of chain and the longest warp you possess.

Make the end fast on board then row away as far as you can, paying out as you go. Drop the anchor so that it makes around 30° with the bower cable.

Consider rowing out a second anchor if you're not going to be swinging to tide or current

97 THE SWEETEST OF GYBES

Gybing a yacht below 40 ft or so in a light breeze, it is generally a waste of effort to pull in the mainsheet. Just gathering the parts and manhandling the boom across is perfectly safe. As the wind picks up, however, you'll need to take precautions. Steer 10° or so off dead downwind, then heave the mainsheet right in and make it fast. Now gybe carefully to a similar angle on the other side of the breeze. As the boom flops across, the boat will tend to luff. The trick of a sweet gybe is to counteract this with a nudge of 'opposite helm' to stop the boat's tendency to round up. When things have stabilised, ease the mainsheet to trim for the new course. If it's really windy, you'll have to let out the sheet smartly to keep control.

A tip for an easy gybe

98 HELP YOUR CREW

Always try to steer through a tack rather than just shoving the helm over and hoping for the best. If you go about too sharply, the jib-sheet handlers will have a tough job winding in the genoa. Life will be far easier if, after coming through the wind, you hold the boat 10° or so above close-hauled while they bring in the sheet, then fill away onto your new course. The team will love you and the boat will tack more efficiently.

Steer through a tack to help your crew

99   A SHORTER SCOPE

It is well known that three or four times the maximum expected depth of water is a good starting point for deciding scope when anchoring with chain cable. This rule is not cast in stone, however. You might safely opt for less cable if you are tight for space, your anchor seems well set, conditions are not extreme and you will be aboard at High Water. This can be useful when room is tight and the tide is due to fall during the night, because you know your scope will increase before it begins to decrease again. If your anchor holds at bedtime, it should do so until morning.

Less anchor cable is an option if you are tight for space

100   NO HOOKS ON THE LEECH

Few abominations can compare with a 'motoring leech', but the leech line should really be the last resort in subduing the horror. If you over-tighten the line, it will end up by 'hooking' the leech of the sail and ruining the clean airflow off its trailing edge. Before attending to the leech line, first make sure the sheet's fairlead car is correctly set in its fore-and-aft position; now ease the line until it is slack, then carefully pull it down until the leech goes quiet, *and not an inch more*.

If you have had to give a reefed mainsail a touch of leech line, don't forget to let it off as you shake out the reef.

Check your genoa car positions before you start pulling leech lines

101 TO SPRING OR NOT TO SPRING?

Midships cleats are very useful in marinas for rigging lines that prevent the boat from surging fore and aft. These are not true spring lines, however. Boat 'B' is rigged marina fashion, while Boat 'A' is rigged with real springs. These have two advantages:

1. Bring in all lines, then motor astern against the spring led from the quarter and the bow will lift off the dock as if by magic (vice versa the bow spring). This doesn't work properly with a midships spring.
2. Where a boat persists in lying 'bows-in' despite all you do, a heave on the stern spring will tuck the quarter in sweetly in a way a midships spring can never achieve.

With real springs   Marina fashion

Boat A is secured alongside with 'real' springs

102 MAINSAIL TWIST – THE SIMPLE TEST

When applying kicking strap or mainsheet tension to control the leech twist of a conventional mainsail, the question arises as to how hard you should be pulling. In the context of a cruising yacht, the answer is as simple as this: heave down until the top batten of the sail lines up parallel with the boom when sighted from underneath it. The curve of the mainsail leech will then generally follow that of the genoa, giving rise to a good-looking rig that is working efficiently.

The leech should be looking sweet when the top batten is parallel with the boom

103   WHEN THE GOING GETS TOUGH

It's all very well imagining that a roller genoa is the answer to all our prayers. It certainly makes life easier in light and moderate going, but when the big winds blow, most of them set like a retired Spillers flour bag – unlike this Twister, which is powering along with a small hanked-on jib and loving every minute of it. Consider having a second forestay fitted to fly smaller sails, including storm sails. If you're going out and think you may be in for a pounding, you can always hank a smaller headsail on in port and tie it down well to the deck. It'll be there if you need it and there'll be no dragging of sail bags along heaving decks.

A small jib is just the job in a blow

104   PUMP HER IN

When a moored boat must be hove in closer to the dock, it's a lot easier to grab the bight (the middle) of a rope that's made fast ashore, then heave up on it while a mate on board holds it with a turn on a cleat. When the boat is significantly shifted, take off the strain quickly while the crew aboard snatches up the slack. Trying to heave the weight in from behind a guardrail is a tough job.

A useful technique for bringing a boat closer in

105 GIVE THEM THE END

When rafting up alongside another yacht, you often have to pass a line to someone on board her. There is a tendency to give the other crew a long length of rope, then ask them to feed it around a cleat somehow and pass it back to you. This fixation on rigging everything as a slip-line can cause no end of messing around. It is far easier to run your lines as big ships do.

Hand a loop or a bowline across and say, "Please drop this over your cleat and we'll deal with it". If you've come in neatly, your crew have then only to snap in the slack and make the bight fast on their own boat. If you've screwed up and the yacht needs a heave in, at least it will be your own people who are doing the pulling and not some innocent bystander. You can always rig slip ropes when it's time to leave – the chances are you won't have to.

Don't pass handfuls of line ashore. Opt for a simple bowline and take up the slack onboard

106 AGROUND!

When you are aground and struggling to heel the boat over so as to reduce her draught, a handy method is to swing the boom as far out as it will go with a crew volunteer hanging onto the end – the heavier the better. If there are no takers for the job, a 20-litre water can is sometimes almost as effective.

Don't just stand there! Get the crew onto the end of the boom if you get stuck in the mud

107   HALYARD TENSION

You can't really tell whether a main halyard is pulled up hard
enough by wiggling the luff in your hand. The only certain way is
to examine the sail once it's set. A mainsail should have its centre
of curvature (its maximum 'camber') just forward of halfway aft
from the luff. A headsail's should be about 35% of the way aft.
This aspect of the shape of either sail is largely controlled by the
halyard. More tension shifts the camber forward. Less allows it
to pull aft. It's common to find a roller headsail with inadequate
tension. Look for wrinkles running across it from the luff as well
as the general shape. For some sails, this may mean more tension
on a windy day and less when the breeze is light. The only way to
find out is to experiment.

**The sail's centre of curvature can be moved forward or aft
by adjusting halyard tension**

108   A CLEAN TOW

The towing boat in this picture had a problem because of
her self-steering – it wouldn't
take much of a tweak from a
towrope to bend something.
She therefore rigged a simple
towing bridle, a good idea on
any boat with a stern-hung
rudder. Using a bridle in any
situation is a kindness because
it spreads the load between
at least two points. Rig it so
you can always slip one end.
Secure the towrope to the bridle with a bowline and cleat
it off on the towed vessel so
either yacht can let go in an
emergency.

A towing bridle spreads the load

109   HULL SPEED

Many modern yachts have very powerful engines. This one is using hers to travel at hull speed – or flat out. You can tell she can't go faster by checking out the huge hollow in the wave form along her hull.

It's tempting to 'give it heaps' when you've revs to spare, but a boat gulps down much more fuel at hull speed than she does at three-quarters of this magic figure. That's also around the best speed a typical yacht can make close-hauled, so there's a useful guide. She'll create dramatically less wash, so the harbourmaster will be pleased, too.

The hollow in the wave form along her hull indicates she's reached hull speed

110   STALLING THE MAIN

A useful guide to setting up the mainsheet traveller is to close-haul the sail with the sheet, then bring the car up to weather until the luff stops lifting. In light weather, it can be acceptable to heave it all the way across until the boom is right on the midships line, but if the spar is allowed to come to windward of this critical setting, then weather helm and slow boat speed will be your portion. In a stronger breeze, a main set to weather of amidships like this one can leave the boat broaching when she's hard on the wind.

A main set to weather of amidships can cause the boat to broach when hard on the wind

111 BACK UP TO THE GALE

If you try to come alongside a wall conventionally in a strong offshore gale, you'll struggle to get anyone ashore. As you lose way the keel stalls and a modern yacht with a cut-away profile blows off to leeward in short order. One solution is to nose up to the dock and have someone climb off the pulpit with a couple of lines. The problem is that most sailing boats, left to themselves, end up with their bows at about 150 degrees to the wind. They prefer, therefore, to back up to the wall with a fender rigged. Have a nimble crew member ready on the transom – the sugar scoop's ideal if you have one – and come slowly in astern until they can step off. It's easier than you think because the helm is close to the action and the boat wants to do what you're asking of her. Get a short stern line on, then run a long line to the bow and lead it via a fairlead to a windlass or winch. The rest is easy.

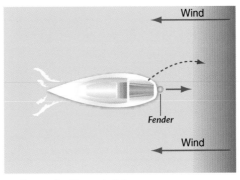

Modern yachts like to do it in reverse ...

112 VARIABLE DRAUGHT

Here's one for bilge-keeled boat owners. It's easy to forget that a twin-keeler's draught increases as she heels over, possibly by as much as a foot. This is worth bearing in mind next time you're tempted to nip across a shallow sandbank with the sails hauled in tight.

When a bilge-keeler heels, her draught increases

113 FLUTTER CLUTTER

A fluttering leech makes a racket like a helicopter, it wears out the sail and it ditches air that could be helping the cause of progress. Most of us don't flinch from adjusting the genoa leech line, but the main can be more of a challenge. The clew may be hard to get at, or out of reach altogether, and the wretched thing often demands attention after reefing. A decent sail will have its leech line exposed with a jamming cleat at each reef. As soon as the fluttering starts, clip on and go climbing. Heave the line down and slip the bight into the cleat. Boats with high booms may have the leech line led via the head of the sail to the tack, for easier access.

A decent mainsail with an easily adjustable leech line at each reef

114 SLOUGH IT OFF

Anyone who regularly picks up a mooring under sail knows that when a yacht rounds up through 180° with no drive on, the braking effect of her rudder drags off a surprising amount of way. It's worth bearing this in mind if you find yourself needing to slow down with no astern propulsion to help you. Modern yachts have big rudders. Whacking one back and forth as far as you can might make you look like a lunatic, but you won't seem so daft when you step on to the dock to bring her up sweetly with the stern line than if you'd done nothing and piled in at 5 knots. If things are really dire, you could even try a 'three-sixty'. As with all unorthodox manoeuvres, have a go before you need it, and choose a day when nobody's looking!

Spin the wheel to slow the boat

115 AMIDSHIPS FOR PEACE

People with tillers generally lash them amidships when they're anchored or moored in a tideway. It stops the boat surging around and helps her drift clear of any optimists who have brought up closer than you'd have wished. Keeping the stick in the middle also makes a big difference to the folks on the foredeck trying to secure a mooring. If the rudder's across the stream, the poor souls will be fighting all the way. This is far less obvious on a wheel-steered boat, so make sure the helm is clearly marked and lock it amidships before you call it a day.

Lock the wheel amidships at anchor

116 HEEL HER OFF

When you're aground and the tide is a long time coming (or worse), if all else has failed, try attaching a rope to a spare mast-head halyard. The angle of heel this can produce is dramatic and may well lessen your draught sufficiently to do the business. If you can't muster a handy RIB like this chap, run your line to a mooring or lay out an anchor and hitch the halyard to the kedge, then crank the halyard in and watch her crunch off sideways. A drastic situation can sometimes justify drastic methods.

Heeling her off with a spare masthead halyard – a last-ditch solution for a dangerous situation

117   WHEN IN DOUBT, DROP THE MAIN

Once in a while, we all are inclined to sail onto a mooring or the anchor. The big issue is this:

- Wind and tide together? Fine. Come in under mainsail – plus jib if you feel like it.
- Wind against tide? – No doubt about this one either. Drop the main. If you leave it up, you'll never stop. Alternatively, you'll luff up, grab the buoy or sling the pick, only to see the tide swing you round and gybe you. Very uncomfortable. So drop the main and approach under headsail only.
- Wind across tide? Hmm. Not sure, really? The only answer is: 'When in doubt, drop the main'. Do that and all will be sweetness and light. Keep it up, take an unkind wind shift, and consternation is your portion!

Sailing onto a mooring – but which sail to keep up?

118   DECENT SHORELINES

To be able to do its job in any circumstances, a dock line on any but the largest cruising yacht should be at least the length of the boat. You need four of these, one for each function. A couple of even longer ones are useful for rafting up and all those odd contingencies you can't predict. In marinas, full-length lines can be a nuisance, so chop the best bits out of an old one to use as short fore and aft breast ropes on tidy pontoons.

Your lines should be at least as long as your boat

119   DON'T FORGET THE LADDER

Securing against a high wall, one of the biggest problems is that the lines must be so long to reach the dock that, as the tide rises, the boat swings out awkwardly. Making use of a convenient ladder is good news, so long as you've given it a survey and it looks man enough for the job. You can reach it easily, so you can shift the rope's position up or down a rung or two without having to put down your mug of tea. In practice, because it's attached at neither top nor bottom, the line may well not need shifting at all. A ring set into the wall is equally handy, and has the advantage of not upsetting a fussy harbourmaster.

A line to a ladder stops her swinging out

120   FLIP THE FENDERS IN

It's a sensible policy to rig warps and fenders in good time. Sailing along with them over the side well before you arrive is not so bright, however. It exposes them needlessly to the wash of your progress, and it looks terrible. The answer is to rig them ready, then flip them inside the guardrails on to the sidedecks. As the crew go forward to take the dock lines ashore, they've only to kick them under the wires and anyone can tell you know what you're doing.

Don't let them dangle!

121 FENDERS PORT SIDE!

Most marinas have berths from hell. 'Z26' may be a plum spot at High Water slack, but as soon as the ebb gets going it could guarantee an insurance claim if you so much as ease one of your springs. Walled, 'artificial' marinas are generally relatively free of practical jokes except in strong crosswinds, but any berth in a river or near a lock must be treated with suspicion.

Eyeball the odds when you come in and imagine what'll be happening when you plan to leave. Try to be head-up to any current, and always be on the lookout for the dreaded cross-set. Accept that some berths, at some times, cannot be safely entered or left.

A cross-tide conundrum?

122 FLAKE TO RUN FREE

The mainsheets is a constant challenge to the sailor who loves a tidy cockpit. This skipper has had his sailmaker run up a neat zip-up bag, which keeps it out of the way. The crew has been zealous with the coil so it will probably run off OK, but if it had been flaked into the bag you'd be happier dumping the sheet in a hurry.

Flaked into a bag

123　A MIND OF HER OWN

Long-keeled yachts with their rudders hung from the keel itself –
or a long fin with a skeg for that matter – have a well-deserved
reputation for being hard to handle astern under power. It's easy
just to say, "There's nothing I can do – she has a mind of her
own," but this is almost never true. Given flat water, no wind and
no current, any boat will perform the same antics every time, so
long as the helm and revs are equal. The trick is to wait for this
rarity, grab it, and find out what she really prefers doing.

Your only task is then to consider how real-life conditions will
affect these natural tendencies. If there's some manoeuvre she
won't perform at any price, don't ask her. Look for another way,
wait for the tide to turn, or go somewhere else in the first place.
And if you think you're hard done by, spare a thought for the skipper of this old pilot cutter!

Long-keeled yachts can be hell to motor astern

124　KEEP 'EM CLEAR

When a number of boats raft up, an issue often arises about
shorelines chafing on bows or quarters. Try leading a lighter line
around the bight of the offending shoreline like this, and heaving
it up just enough to clear the lead.

Change the lead of shorelines if needed

125 TOWING SPEED

If you're ever unfortunate enough to need a tow, watch out for over-enthusiastic motorboat drivers. A sailing yacht should not be towed at much above a speed equivalent to the square root of her waterline length (around 5 knots for 30 ft on deck). At this speed she is easy to steer and makes little resistance to progress. At 'hull speed' (around 1.4 x the square root of LWL in feet), she is flat-out. Even a single knot faster is going to strain things mightily. It's not easy to ask a fisherman engaged in saving your ship to slow down, but it's worth a try. Mention it politely while you're passing the towline rather than waiting until your cleats start pulling out.

Lifeboats have bulletproof gear. Yachts don't!

126 HOLDING STATION

Holding station in a strong breeze, it's only natural to try to hang in head-to-wind. In fact, most modern yachts don't like this. Left to themselves they tend to end up with the wind over the quarter. It is far less stressful to let the bow blow off the breeze, then hold position by going slow astern every so often to keep her right where you want her.

Let the bow blow off the breeze

127   BURY IT BEHIND THE MAIN

When something goes wrong on the foredeck, the natural instinct of most sailors is to luff up head-to-wind. This often does us no favours. It puts strain on the forestay as everything comes on the shake, and it increases the apparent wind. If the boat can be run off instead, the headsail – be it a genoa whose roller gear is playing up, or a cruising chute gone temporarily mad – will be sheltered in the wind shadow of the mainsail. This collapses it and leaves it docile. There's no stressful clattering about and the apparent wind drops magically as well, so there's less chance of general damage.

Bear away and blanket the headsail with the main

128   HANG 'EM HIGH

Approaching any alongside situation – especially a raft-up – don't assume anything where fenders are concerned. Hang them too low for a motorboat with flared topsides and they might as well have stayed in the locker. The same holds good with another sailing boat if she's a different size. Always take a good long look at what you'll be lying against before committing to fender height. A simple clove hitch on the top guardrail ensures easy adjustment if you get it wrong.

Take a good look before committing to fender height

129 THE MIGHTY BULL ROPE

Here's a very useful anchoring lash-up. It's used primarily by folks who sail gaffers, but could be equally effective for anyone with a stout spinnaker pole and the means to tie it down securely to the bow roller and foredeck. When you're anchored with wind against tide, rig a block or bullseye to the end of the bowsprit or pole and run a line through it with both ends led back on board. Bring one part in through the anchor fairlead or roller and secure it to the cable on deck. Now let go another fathom or two of cable, so that the knot is under water. Heave on the other part and pull the bight of the chain up towards the bowsprit. As the boat surges forward under the windage of her rig, she will lie to this 'bull rope' instead of having the chain graunch all the way around the stem, mashing the topsides into the grisly bargain.

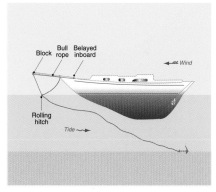

A bull rope on a sprit or pole saves your topsides

130 TURN IT UP

When you need the safety of a turn on a winch, maintain a whole turn-and-a-half, not half a turn. The sheet will pull in fast without riding turns, and it's easy to whip off, too. In this photo, there is already half a turn and the deck-hand is about to put another turn on – proper job.

Take a whole turn-and-a-half instead of just a half a turn when sheeting in

131   FAIRLEADS AND SLIPLINES

Fairleads are often sited awkwardly for handling stern lines. Even if they started life well intentioned, it's a pound to a penny that by the time you arrive on the scene they will be shrouded with safety gear and GPS aerials. Leave them out of the equation when running your lines. You can always jam the bight in later if need be.

Keep fairleads out of the equation when slipping lines

132   FACE UP TO KEEPING WAY ON

Shaping up for a gap in a tight raft, it takes nerve to keep plenty of way on but, if you chicken out, the keel will stall and the boat will start going sideways. That's the beginning of the end, so hang in there and give her enough gas to maintain control.

The most effective way to keep control of a boat going astern is to face the way she is going. Sit alongside the console if she has one and drive her like a car.

Drive her like a car!

133 SLIP SAFELY IN

It's tempting to rig every fender you've got when entering a raft, but this may not be the best bet. As you squeeze in you can almost guarantee yours will hang up on the neighbours'. At worst, they'll snag badly and ruin your manoeuvre. Rig them ready, don't be in a hurry to kick them over, and keep a roving fender ready for all eventualities. It's absolutely okay to lie gently against neighbouring boats for support as you enter a raft. Using them as well-fendered cushions on either side makes the job even easier. Just squeeze in politely, then rig your lines.

Mind your fenders don't get tangled

134 HEY, BIG FENDER!

Laying up for the winter, you can take away all the worry of gales blowing onto the berth by suspending a big fender fore-and-aft from the pontoon cleats. Then when the boat heels towards the berth she can't 'duck under' her usual fenders. It also takes the strain off guardrails and stanchions. Secured in the right place with the yacht's lines all sorted, it will handle all the load, leaving its smaller sisters with no more than backup duty. If it's too big to stow on board, so much the better. When spring comes around, stuff it in the garage loft to wait for its moment of glory next November.

The big fender takes all the load, leaving the others as a backup

135   GIVE HER SOME AIR

When the wind's so light your pipe smoke goes straight up (or it used to, before having fun was banned), any decent boat with a clean bottom will still sail. She won't go anywhere, however, if her sails are flat. So ease those halyards and outhauls, give the close-hauled sheets 6 inches of slack, back off the kicker and don't try to point too high. Oh yes, and sit anyone spare to leeward to induce an angle of heel. That way the sails will drop into shape and what breeze there is won't squander its energy trying to blow the sails into the right shape!

Ghosting along with sails slackened

136   BACKING OFF

When you run aground in mud going ahead, the first option is to try motoring off directly astern, following the groove you've just dug. However, if you're well stuck, it's worth knowing that most gear-box-propeller combinations don't deliver so much oomph astern as they do ahead. If all seems lost, try putting the helm hard over and swivelling the boat by throwing water against the rudder with the engine full ahead. You may persuade her to swing far enough round to thrash off making the most of the engine's grunt.

Stuck in the mud? Sometimes using forward power can be the answer

ROPES AND KNOTS

137 COILS OF ROPE

Most of us make up coils for stowing by using some variant of the gasket coil hitch. This does a neat job by wrapping one end around the whole coil a few times. Sadly, some dock lines and kedge warps are too big to achieve this conveniently. A good compromise is to clove hitch one end around the coil as shown. It needs a bit of practice, but once you've mastered it you can say goodbye to the snake's wedding in your rope locker.

Use a clove hitch when coiling long ropes – it will help keep your lockers tidy

138 FRESHEN THAT NIP

Chafe is the great enemy of the far-voyaging sailing vessel. From clipper ship to mini-yacht it's the same old problem. Even on short runs, especially downwind, some rope somewhere is going to suffer damage from a nasty lead. This one has been worrying away at the cheek of its snatch block. The ideal answer is to rearrange the lead, but that's not always possible. Sailing ships used to ease their halyards and sheets an inch or two every day, then sweat them up every so often to 'freshen the nip' in the sheaves. That's what has been done here, and the rope will live to fight again – just.

This rope has been chafing on the snatch block

139   ALL SET?

Crew like to be told what's happening. If the hands are well briefed, the skipper is in with a far better chance of not making a 'Horlicks' out of a berthing manoeuvre. Instead of saying, "I think we'll go over there..." try something like this: "Okay! We'll try the second finger down in that gap – just past the pink motorboat. Portside-to, fenders as low as you can get them – on deck for now and kick 'em over when we're nearly there. Bow line and stern spring, please. Make the bights fast aboard, hop off when you safely can, secure to the cleats on the dock and we'll tidy up once we're secure."

Keep the crew well briefed

140   STRESS-FREE HOME-PORT BERTHING

There's usually one critical line to get ashore when you return to your home berth and far too often the job can be a night-mare, particularly in marinas beset with tidal streams. The whole business of someone having to leap ashore and grab a turn can be removed with this setup. The vital first permanent shoreline is secured to the relevant cleat, then the bight is laid through a row-lock mounted on a stalk of some sort. All the crew need do is stand by the appropriate cleat on board, lift the rope off as they go by, bend down and make it up. No jumping, and less stress for the skipper too. If the yacht's a foot too far out, they can still reach it with the boathook, so long as they keep one handy for those days when the helmsman is off form.

A rowlock on a stick presents a shoreline

141 A LONG BOWLINE

You might be forgiven for thinking this was going to be a tip about not securing to rotten tree stumps, but it isn't. The point to be made is that a bowline with a big loop was used, not a round turn and two half hitches. This is because the crew wanted to be able to flip the line clear when the time came, no matter how hard the wind was blowing. The same holds good if securing to a ring on a pile in a tidal situation. If you're unlucky and the ring jams at the bottom of the iron stay when the tide rises, it can end up out of reach. Anyone who's used a short knot is left high and dry. A long bowline will always make it to the surface.

A use for long bowlines

142 GIVE IT SOME SLACK

A heap of dinghies like this is an offence to God and man. Either yours is on the inside and you can't get it out, or it's been left with plenty of slack and you can only reach it by clambering through two or three others, likely full of water. It's easy to blame the harbour authority for not supplying sufficient dock footage, but users can help one another by leaving their boats on the longest painter they can muster. A minimum of 15 ft will give enough manoeuvring room for everyone to shuffle their punt alongside. Any 'me-first' sailors found tying up short for their own convenience should be frogmarched to the beach, hung with their painters and left between high and low water. Napoleon used a similar technique and he knew all about discipline.

Always leave about 15 ft of slack in your painter when making fast to a pontoon

143 KEEP COILS TURNING WITH THE SUN

Braidline rope with a braid core can be coiled clockwise or anti-clockwise, but three-strand line rope is only happy if it is turning 'with the sun', or clockwise. This is to do with the construction of the lay of the rope. To force it anti-clockwise creates excessive kinks. You may get away with it on a short length, but it's bad practice. Try it on a schooner's 200 ft peak halyard and you'll be sorry when the mate finds out it was you who caused the sail to jam halfway down!

When coiling three-strand rope, make sure you coil it clockwise so that it goes with the lay

144 DIPPING YOUR LOOPS

Where more than one rope must be made up on a shoreside cleat or bollard, always pass the loop of the second and subsequent lines through the loop that was there first. The geometry of this is hard to explain, but the result is that no matter what loads are on the ropes, when you slack one away you will always be able to lift it clear. This seamanlike solution is a far happier answer than wrestling with the made-up bight of a single line doing duty as a pair of springs.

This simple technique should make untangling mooring lines easier

145 A HITCH IN TIME

Cow-hitching the coil of the genoa furling line to a guardrail is a great way to stow it on any boat that's not too huge. If you're right-handed and the line is on the port side, as it often is, the natural way to make it up is with the bight on the outboard side of the guardrail. If you hitch it up so the bight is inside like this, all you need do to release it is grab the bight and pull.

One tug and the line is released

146   CAREENING IN THE TWENTY-FIRST CENTURY

Sailing with a foul bottom is hateful to us all, but how many would go to the lengths of these young Frenchmen to maintain performance? They've run a halyard ashore from the masthead, sorted out their lines and fenders, then hauled the boat over so they can get at the bottom, and a fine job they're making of it, too. Everyone used to do this with full-sized sailing ships in the great age of sail, but in today's Britain you'd have to post a lookout to warn of lurking health and safety officers. If your risk assessment doesn't stack up, you could just heel her enough to get nicely below the waterline. What a difference even that would make.

Heel her over for a good scrubbing

147   POP A PILL

Being seasick is miserable and can often be avoided by taking a couple of seasickness tablets. Don't wait until you or your crew are feeling queasy or reaching for a bucket before taking the pills. Take the recommended dose before you go to sleep to allow the drugs to get into your system and then take another dose the following morning. If you are worried about getting drowsy, have a trial run on dry land well before your cruise so that you know how you are likely to react.

Pre-emptive strike against seasickness

148   KEEPING YOUR BITS AND PIECES

This man and his dog are fixing the head in a foreign marina. It's ten-to-one he won't have the spare he needs, but fortunately he has a serious tool kit and he's shipped a load of assorted bits and pieces. If a diesel injector goes down, there may be no cure except a reconditioned one, but many gear failures can be cobbled up with the most unlikely items of hardware. All tiny nuts, bolts and screws nestling in the boatyard dirt should be pocketed and stowed aboard, no matter how irrelevant they seem; so should pinless shackles, lengths of brass strip, springs of obscure origin, short lengths of armoured piping, washers, a bicycle inner tube, any item of plumbing and, most important of all, a bent wire coat hanger.

Those nuts, bolts and lengths of brass you've been hoarding may come in useful one day

149   NOTHING LASTS FOR EVER

Here's a shiny new syphon breaker in the engine cooling line before the water is injected into the exhaust system. Most yachts have them, and they don't last for ever. It's there for a good reason, and if it fails, an engine-full of water may result. It costs nothing to inspect it every year and clean its valve. If in doubt, it won't break the bank to replace it, then sleep easy all night long.

Check the syphon valve

150   BLEEDING OBVIOUS

You don't have to be a mechanical genius to know that if you run out of diesel or the engine stops because of a clogged filter, you are probably going to have to bleed it to get it going again. Most modern engines bleed from the engine fuel filter, which is often found high up on the block, as this one is. Crack the nut at the top as shown. Open it a turn or so, then follow the diesel line towards the tank from the filter until you come to a small pump low down on the side of the engine with a handle sticking out of it. It will probably be the next fitting you reach. Pump this handle up and down and you'll see bubbly diesel coming out from under the nut. Keep pumping until the diesel runs out clear of air, then tighten the nut. Now crank the engine as if you mean it and with any luck it'll start.

Bleed the engine from its fuel filter

151   HANG 'EM HIGH!

Storing fresh fruit and vegetables is always an issue at sea. A sound plan is to rig up some netting around the galley. This frees up locker space, keeps the victuals well aired and allows regular easy checks to toss out any rotters. It also adds a picturesque, workmanlike quality to the accommodation.

Hang your fresh food from your deckhead

152 LOOK OUT FOR THE COOK

Safety equipment doesn't always come pre-packed and labelled with an MCA sticker. More accidents happen in the galley of the average cruising yacht than ever occur from crew tumbling over the side – and they don't all involve fire and gas explosion. A cook is far more likely to be scarred for life by a boiling pot jumping off the stove or a dish that takes charge when a poorly designed oven decants its contents over the crouching galley slave.

The only real protection against such grim contingencies is to wear oilskin bottoms for cooking when it's rough. If the weather's so hot that you can't bear the discomfort, just think 'spills' all the time. Consider the poor skipper as well. There's nothing worse for his morale than those screams from down below . . .

Wear oilskin bottoms for cooking when it's rough

153 BE KIND TO YOUR BEST FRIEND

When it comes to cruising, a man's best friend isn't his dog, it's his engine. Diesel auxiliaries build up acids in old sump oil. Leave the stuff in there all winter and these acids munch away at the engine's vitals, so the best policy is to change the oil in autumn. While you're at it, replace the filter as well. Most modern units make these jobs easy for an owner to manage, and many yards have oil disposal facilities. It'll be one less task at fitting-out time, too.

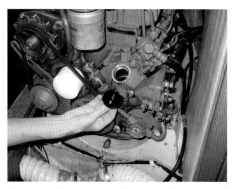

Changing oil at laying-up time does a lot to extend the life of the engine

154 DUTCH TREAT

If you've cruised the Dutch inland waters or the Baltic Sea, you'll have noticed how well the boat sails when you come out again. Your bottom is as clean as a butcher's slab at opening time, because any incipient growth from the ocean loses interest in life as soon as it smells the sweet rivers. It takes a week or 10 days for the full effect. Even if you aren't lucky enough to visit such exotic locations it's still worth knowing, because if you've a chance to lay up for a fortnight inside a lock, you can offset the docking costs against the price of that mid-season scrub you won't be needing.

Dirty bottom? Lock in and let fresh water kill the barnacles

155 WATCH THE AMPS

Some modern plotters are so power hungry that their backs are designed to dissipate heat. While this offers the useful option of using them as toasters if the global GPS signal should fail, it also means we flatten our batteries in short order if we give them their heads. This situation can be eased by searching the system for all available means of saving power. These might include turning the backlight well down when the screen is not in direct use, and keeping an associated radar scanner shut down when you aren't looking at the radar display. Some radars default to 'standby' and are therefore secretly guzzling amps when we might prefer them 'off'.

Plotters can guzzle a lot of power

156   FIXING THE FLAPPING

Modern fractional rigs with tall, narrow, self-tacking jibs are a joy to sail upwind. Unfortunately, many of these otherwise excellent headsails become unsheetable when you ease off onto a reach using only the gear supplied. The sheet position does not allow enough downward pull to compensate for the extreme twist such high-aspect ratio sails experience. The answer is to rig what racers call a 'barber-hauler'. Ideally, attach a single block to the rail, abeam or immediately abaft the jib sheet traveller. Snap-shackle a line to the clew of the sail and lead it through the block aft to a spare winch. Pull down on the clew just enough to settle the sail and that's it. If there's nowhere on the rail, you'll have to contrive something else. If nothing is possible, write to the boatbuilder and demand a retro-fit solution. It is not tolerable to sail along with a shaking leech.

Use a barber-hauler on a reach

157   STOW THE BOARDS

Is your boat one of the majority where the builder hasn't thought about what you're going to do with the companionway wash-boards when they aren't in place? Why not invest one Saturday morning next winter knocking up a thin, open-topped compartment in a big cockpit locker, to drop them into? The incumbent of the quarterberth will bless you the next time he turns in and they aren't sticking into his soft parts.

Well worth investing in a washboard container

158 GET SHOT OF IT

Nothing is so vile as a 150 % genoa with a low-cut clew when it's reefed well in. These sails are designed for Mediterranean boats, which habitually cruise in light airs. In the higher latitudes of home waters, we spend much of our time under short canvas. A 110 % sail will stand without a reef in breezes that would beggar a partly rolled 'big boy'. So long as it's well cut, it will deliver a surprising amount of power in Force 2 as well. Next time you're walking the long, lonesome road to the sailmaker's, consider ordering a sail appropriate to local needs.

A 110 % genoa is ideal for sailing in home waters

159 A PIECE OF STRING

Hands up the sailor who has never dropped a vital shackle pin into the water. The most common victims are halyard shackles, which have to be undone and done up every time the sail is handled. Often hands are cold and the vital pin slips through the fingers – and then why oh why does it always roll over the side? One answer is a captive pin shackle, but if your pin can part company with its parent, try hitching a length of string between it and the shackle, the thimble or even the end of the halyard itself. The string twists, of course, as you screw in the pin, but better that than the alternative.

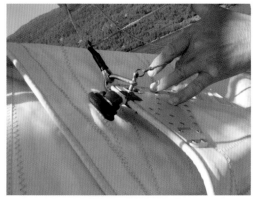

A small piece of string stops the pin escaping

160　SHOVE IT IN

The most common reason for a yacht diesel failing to start relates to when it was last shut down. If it has a 'pull stop' device (usually a toggle on the end of a 'push–pull' cable), it's easy to forget to shove this all the way back in after pulling it out to stop the motor. If the engine whips over but refuses to fire when you turn the key, this is the first place to look. Make sure it's all the way home. Engines with electrical stop devices rely on an electrical solenoid to do the job. Find this at the injector pump and identify the wiring while it's working well. Then, if the engine won't catch even though the starter's whipping it over like a spinning top, you'll know where to start looking.

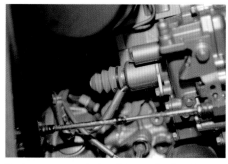

Engine won't start? First thing to check is the stop mechanism

161　DON'T OVERDO THE TENSION

An 8 inch screwdriver is sufficient leverage for setting up the bottlescrews on all but the largest of yachts. Over-tightening can do serious damage to the rig, and the modest lever provides a self-limiting check on your own enthusiasm.

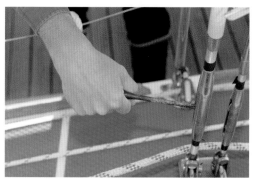

Beware damaging your rig by over-tightening

162   A CLEAN CUT

Every sailor should carry
a knife. You never know
when you'll need it. This
one has a locking blade and
a rather natty little torch,
but it's the blade that
counts. Serrated blades
tackle rope the best. This
half-and-half arrangment
is a good compromise. The
hole in the blade provides

A knife is a vital item of sailing kit

purchase to allow you to open it with one hand – useful if you're
clinging to a thrashing genoa clew with the other. Most importantly, it locks, so it'll never fold up and slice your fingers instead
of the offending rope.

163   BUTTON UP

Anecdotal evidence suggests that more reading glasses and
mobile phones have been lost by sailors leaning down to attend
to a dockline than by any other cause. The only answer is to make
a habit of buttoning that shirt pocket before bending down, or
removing anything from it that could possibly fall out under the
influence of gravity. You might think this is so obvious it's not
worth mentioning, but we recently witnessed a full-time harbourmaster having his day ruined by that sickening 'plop'.

**Don't have your day ruined – button
up that shirt pocket!**

164 A GALLON OF REGULAR AIN'T WHAT IT USED TO BE

Some things in life seem eternal – like the west wind, the cycles of the tide and the explosive nature of a decent gallon of petrol.

The news, however, is that while we can still rely on the breeze and the reversing stream, a tankful of modern petrol that's been sitting in the outboard all winter may well prove little more combustible than a pint of beer. If your dinghy motor won't start when you try it this spring, dump last season's unleaded into the nearest safe disposal unit and refill it with lively new fuel, this year's vintage. Buy it from a busy roadside filling station because the stuff's like real ale – the more they sell, the better it gets. One pull, and you'll be away.

Fresh fuel should see you off with a roar this spring

165 RECYCLE THE NEWSPAPER AND TAKE A SNAP

When you're faced with an intricate job with lots of small parts, circlips and springs, take your time and always lay a sheet of newspaper under the job. It's one thing stripping something on the bench at home but, on board, the bit you want will fall into the cockpit grating and if your luck's really out, it'll go down the drain as well. The paper will catch the lot.

And while you're at it, take a series of digital photos of what went where, so you know how to put it back together again . . .

Spread out a newspaper to catch stray washers

166   DROPPING THE BUCKET

When you need a bucketful of seawater, make sure the handle has a longish lanyard. Tie it to the boat because under way the pull can be considerable. To grab a decent fill every time, don't just drop the bucket in and hope for the best. Instead, gently lob it rim-down into the sea and tip it round so it's open to your direction of travel. It can bring you up with a jerk if you aren't careful, but that's where the skill comes in. Flicking it out just as the pull comes on is the mark of a real seaman!

A good bucket is a friend for life

Buy a quality bucket from your local builder's merchant, and choose the smallest. Failing this, try the chandlery, but never be tempted by the lightweight plastic rubbish that's fit only for the kitchen. Go for heavy rubber or a nice canvas one.

167   YAWL OR KETCH?

We all know they both have two masts, the mainmast being ahead of the mizzen and considerably larger, but which boat is which, and how to remember it? The answer is that, in a yacht, the ketch steps her mizzen forward of the rudder post, while the yawl's is abaft it. 'Yawl' rhymes with 'haul', so if you remember that she's hauling her mizzen along behind her, as it were, you'll never be in doubt again.

Note where the mizzen of this handsome gaffer lands on deck. Then check the rudder at the waterline. She's a yawl, for sure!

168 USE YOUR LOAF!

At sea on extended passages, nothing raises morale as much as the smell of baking bread. Some people just like doing it for fun, and it's great after a week or two of bingeing on baguettes. Tips for making a loaf to lust after:

A great morale-booster

- Buy Patricia Jacobs' *Best Bread Book*
- Use dried yeast and make sure it's in date
- Stow the rising dough near the calorifier to keep it warm on a cold day
- Take brown flour with you. It can be tricky to source
- Try not to eat it hot. It'll slice only in doorsteps and won't last a minute!

169 WEIGH THEM UP

This illustration may appear an odd sight, but although the scales don't look much, they're accurate and the cylinder on them is a lifejacket gas bottle. If you're under the illusion that you have to change yours every year, you may be wrong. Examine them closely and you'll see a 'safe weight for operation' in the small print on one end. Take them home and pop them on the kitchen scales. If they're OK, inflate the lifejackets with your lungs to make sure they're tight and leave them overnight. Then deflate, repack and that's it, done. Sometimes they last for years.

Weigh it – you might not need a new one!

170 OTHER PEOPLE'S RULES

It makes obvious sense when crossing the Channel to carry the ship's registration or SSR document, VHF radio licence, insurance documents, and anything that proves you've paid the VAT. Less blatant, but equally important, are the following. The French have rules about them, which the Cus-

The French tricolour courtesy flag

toms have been known to enforce. Some are obvious, some less so.

- A lifejacket for everyone aboard
- An up-to-date flare pack (don't carry out-of-date flares – they're illegal in France)
- Make sure the liferaft (if carried) is serviced and in date. This is mandatory
- Keep a paper log that you can show to boarding officials if asked

171 BEAT THE CHAFE AT ZERO COST

Chafe's a killer. Its specialities are tow ropes where they pass through stemhead fittings or shorelines under heavy load where the boat is moving constantly in a surge. This owner found himself in with a gale blowing and the lines at full stretch. Looking for relief, he toddled over to the skip where he sourced a useful 2 ft length of toilet pipe. He couldn't take the shoreline off, so he cut a slit in the pipe and worked it onto the bight, then shoved it over the fairlead. Bye bye chafe, and no more lines groaning either. A good night's sleep promised for the hands under the foredeck.

Plastic pipe is a low-cost solution to conquering chafe

172 FILL 'ER UP!

These tanks look the way we like to see them – good and full. However, fuel tank gauges have a habit of 'failing dangerous' and many a yacht has had her diesel splutter to an ignominious halt with the gauge still reading encouragingly full. The answer is to run a column in your log book for 'engine'. With 'on' and 'off', fuel fills, oil changes and so on all logged, doing the square thing by the machinery becomes simple. No guesswork or peering at tiny numbers in an 'engine hours' gauge that nobody's ever checked for accuracy. As to fuel consumption, we all should have a fair idea of how many litres we burn in an hour. Given that, the log book, and starting from 'full', we hardly need a gauge at all.

Don't trust the fuel gauge – log your engine hours

173 HANDS FREE

It's surprising how many folks with auto-pilots only use them on passage. It's grand not to have to steer for hour after hour, but it's equally useful to free up an extra hand to stow a sail or prepare lines and fenders, especially for two-up crews. The only thing is that these manoeuvres are

Keep a good watch if you're on auto-pilot inshore

often in more crowded waters, so once you've left the helm to itself it's doubly important to make a point of looking around the boat very frequently indeed.

174   CHAFE PARANOIA

The problem with all fore-and-aft rigs is that squared away off the wind, they suffer chafe on the mainsails from the standing rigging. Unless you're crossing an ocean, the answer for coastal work is simply to make sure the sail won't run against the metal work and wires. Vang it down hard, set up a gybe preventer, then sheet in firmly so that the boom can't move at all. No movement equals no chafe. Things may look a bit ugly, but it's better that way than heaving in the sheet to hard and suffering weather helm all the way to Cherbourg.

Racing crews may be willing to sacrifice their sails in the name of downwind speed, but cruising boats are better off securing the boom

175   A GREENER CUP OF TEA

We're always being told not to waste fuel, so here's a way of saving a gram or two that can make a real difference – to us, if not to the planet. Exchanging gas bottles can be a hassle, so try counting how many strokes on the hand or foot pump it takes to fill a mug, then use exactly the right amount in the kettle. Overfilling wastes a surprising amount of gas over the weeks. If you're unlucky enough not to have a manual pump in the galley, count how many seconds the job takes on the electric one instead. The secret benefit of the manual pump is that you can give it a simple in-line filter and know your tea will taste great every time. It'll last for ages if you keep it for drinking and use the power pump for washing-up.

Save water, save gas and save time in the galley

176 DON'T JUST SAVE IT FOR YOUR CHIPS

A gallon can of malt vinegar costs next to nothing compared with most yacht unctions, yet it has many uses on board. In addition to revitalising a plate of chips rendered beyond salvation by a route march from the local friary, it can also put the shine back into brass that has tarnished far beyond a quick rub up with the magic wadding. If the metal-work is modern rubbish, don't leave it submerged overnight because it may dissolve altogether. A carefully monitored dip is what's required. When your gloss varnish below decks is looking dowdy, mix a little vinegar with water and wipe it down. Dry it off carefully with a clean cloth and it'll come up smiling every time. An egg-cup full down the sink when you leave the boat kills the smells, and the wonderful thing is that although the stuff pongs for a while, it doesn't linger.

Vinegar – not just for chips!

177 AN ELECTRICAL SHIELD

Next time you're caught in an electrical storm, grab your handheld VHF radio and your spare GPS, and pop them in the oven. Shut the door and don't light the gas! Whatever happens to any instruments with masthead antennae, the kit in the cooker will be OK. If you take a strike and lose all the main equipment – you probably will, whether the antennae are connected or not – you'll still be able to communicate by radio and you'll know where you are!

Kit in the cooker will survive a lightning strike

178 TOM AND DICK

If you're going off watch and you're feeling a little 'Tom and Dick' (that's 'seasick' in East London), don't even think about struggling into a bunk up forward that may have your name on it. The best chance you have of survival is to nip below, keep your kit on, and crash in the saloon. The motion is less there and you're straight down into the horizontal mode, which is well-known to be far less sick-making. If the boat is modern and has no seaberths amidships, chuck some cushions on the floor, if there are no sailbags, and crash out on those. Take a large saucepan with you just in case!

Hunker down in the saloon if you're seasick

179 SLIP SLIDING AWAY

In theory, plastic sail slides should rattle up the mast track like the proverbial rat up a drainpipe. The facts of life, especially after a winter lay-up, may be very different. The answer isn't a squirt from the aerosol oil can. This may help the sail go up but it can end up messy and it doesn't last. Crossover technology is the way ahead. Until recently, the best product was a spray of 'dry' silicone lubricant designed to make curtains slip sweetly on their rails. It worked even better on sail slugs. Now, you can buy specialised marine products from your neighbourhood chandler that do the same job, only better, they say. Either can transform hoisting and dropping a sticky mainsail.

180 THE CREEPING IMPELLER BLUES

It's tempting to ignore an engine cooling impeller on the admirable principle that 'if it ain't bust, don't fix it'. Most rules can be proved by examining the exceptions, however, and this is one of them. Over the seasons, and especially during long winter lay-ups, impellers steadily harden so that performance drops off imperceptibly. Blades suffer minor damage, perhaps splitting over half their length, making them more likely to rip off if a blockage runs them dry for a minute or two.

Don't ignore an engine cooling impeller

Check the impeller at the beginning of the season. If it's tired, replace it. If it looks good, at least you know that the screws on the end plate all work. When you need to change it in a hurry on a lee shore, you won't lose your ship because of a stripped thread.

181 A SORRY SIGHT

There's usually a lot that can be done with halyard, sheet, outhaul and kicker to shape up a sad-looking mainsail, but if you find yourself underneath one that looks like this after you've tried all you know, it's time to consign it to the bin and brass up for a new one. Any sail with a camber as 'hard' as this and a leech that's falling away despite the battens and your best efforts is, to put it bluntly, shot. There are a lot of them around . . .

This mainsail is well past its sail-by date!

182 GIVE THE KIDS A LURE

Ever feel bad about trying to sail at two or three knots in light winds while the kids get bored and restless? Here's the answer.

Any time from May onwards, the mackerel start running, and a slow-moving sailing boat is the best vehicle known to man for hooking them out. No special skill needed. You'll have change from £10 when you treat the family to a mackerel trolling line. Invest in a 'trolling board' paravane for an extra £5 and you're in the fast lane, ready to fish at a fathom or so down. If they're there, you'll catch them.

Introduce the kids to fishing

Kids of either sex can really get into the whole business, especially when they eat their catch for supper. They aren't as squeamish as you may be when it comes to gutting, and because there are still enough fish in the sea for your efforts to make little difference to stocks, the job's as green as grass. It's a great yachting tradition. Let's take it on to the next generation.

183 SLEEP WHEN YOU NEED IT

It pays handsomely not to try and fight your metabolism when you're setting watches. If the skipper likes a kip an hour after he's eaten his curry, give him the middle watch from midnight until three and let him sleep in the evening, when it comes naturally to him. Some people have no problem staying awake after they've eaten, so give them the after-dinner watch.

If the skipper likes to kip straight after his curry, give him the 'graveyard shift'

184 LEARN TO DESIGN

Kids playing up after two days in port? Game Boy's batteries flat? Good. Set them the task of designing and building a yacht that will sail across the harbour. This one was created from a polystyrene dish that came from a Breton fishmonger with a *plateau de fruits de mer*. The ballast is water in a supermarket bag, the mast a piece of junk and the rigging is made of twisted duct tape. The sails are superbly cut from a copy of *The Salisbury Journal*, but the trick that conferred vital directional stability was the centreboard. This was fashioned from a strip of baked-bean can, flattened and shoved through the bottom, well abaft

Challenge the kids to build a model boat

the centre of lateral resistance so that it kept her going straight, even downwind. A lesson there for many a designer, especially this rather large child who built the good ship *Fiasco*.

185 BLOOD ON THE DECK

It's always tempting on a hot day to sail barefoot, but there's many a yacht with blood on her decks from nature's children stubbing their toes. A useful compromise is to offer the tootsies to the sun in the cockpit, but keep a pair of easy-on deck shoes handy for trips to the foredeck.

Protect your toes on deck

186   DODGY SUNSET

Here's a proper red sky
and it's at night, prom-
ising sailors a day of
delight after breakfast
in the morning. Actu-
ally, what it shows is
that you can't always
rely on ancient lore. For
the old adage to hold
good, it really needs
a fairly clear sky to go
with it. The one in the
photograph, messy as

**A red sky at night doesn't guarantee
delightful weather in the morning**

it is, came backed up by a falling barometer and lived up to its
ugly looks. It dished up torrential rain overnight that kept going
all the way into the following afternoon. A sky like this in the
morning leaves no doubts. It should have anyone within reach of
a harbour scurrying for cover!

187   BOOT TOP – AESTHETIC OR
        PRAGMATIC?

Look at the boot top on this yacht. The lower interface of the
white line is parallel with the water. The upper one, where it meets
the varnish, sweeps up at the bow, following a shallow parabola
halfway between the curve of the sheer and the waterline. The
vast majority of yacht painters no longer take the trouble to follow this traditional skill. If the yacht has a flattish sheer it doesn't
make much difference, but for a boat with a spring to her looks,
to saddle her with a parallel boot top is to sell her sadly short. Get
it right and she lifts her head up and walks with more of a swing.
It's tricky, but so well worth the trouble.

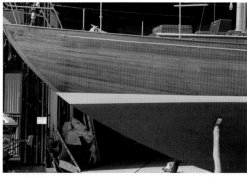

**A carefully upswept boot top enhances this yacht's grace-
ful sheerline**

188 CHEAPEST CHAIN MARKERS

Professional chain markings like these are fine if you can find and afford them. If you've left it too late yet again this year, check along the top shelf in the garage and locate that can of spray touch-up enamel for the car you sold five years ago. The colour doesn't matter because anything except grey shows up. Lay out the chain, grab last week's *Telegraph* to mask the ground or deck, and spray four links for a mark. Keep it very simple:

- One mark at 10 m, because you'll never need less than that.
- Two marks at 20 m. If you want 15 m, get the 20 m mark up on deck. There will be a couple of metres between the windlass or cleat and the water, so that makes 18 m. Pull in a fathom (a full two-arm, 2 m spread) and that's about it.
- Use three marks at 30 m and four at 40 m. If you have more than that, start again with extra-long marks and don't forget to spray a whole metre of the chain before the bitter end pops out . . .

In the absence of chain markers like these, use spray paint

189 LED ALTERNATIVES

Rather than stick with established technology, the owner of this yacht has replaced her standard nav lights with LED alternatives. They're just as bright, if not brighter, with as little as 1.5 W power draw as opposed to 15 W, and if one element should go bust (10,000 hours

LED lights are more expensive, but require less power to run

life expectancy), you've two left to lighten your darkness. They cost more, but some existing lamps can be converted to use LED bulbs.

WEATHER

190 A SPRING IN THE WIND

Some 14 knots of true wind is a good sailing breeze for most of us. If we're beating, 10 knots will do. At 18 knots in open water, many yachts are reefed and their crews are wishing they were going downhill instead.

Now, a brimming spring tide will hit the best part of 4 knots in the middle of the English Channel, which, trundling along under still air, is creating an apparent up-tide wind of 4 knots. Add this to a 14-knot true wind blowing directly up and down the tide – a westerly in the Channel, for example – and an easy 10 knots on the lee-going stream is transformed into a stiff 18 knots when it's flowing hard to weather. The forecast won't mention this, or the change in sea state, but that's another matter . . .

A fair spring tide can significantly increase the apparent wind

191 HALO, HALO

When you see a halo like this around the sun or moon, stand by for dirty weather. We aren't talking about those little ones that fuzz themselves around the heavenly body. These big chaps are sure-fire harbingers of unpleasantness. Watch the barometer. When it starts falling and the wind backs as well, that's you for the high jump. If you're safely anchored, let out all the cable you've got. Far out at sea without the option, reeve up the deep reef pennant, cook a meaty stew, then pray.

Haloes around the sun are sure-fire harbingers of unpleasantness

192 SQUALL!

You can never be sure what'll happen when a cumulonimbus ('cu-nimb') cloud like this comes your way, but you'll be lucky if the answer is 'nothing at all'. If the horizon beneath the ice-cream castle is obscured, you can be sure you'll get rain and probably wind as well. If you see lightning, it's probably classifiable as an isolated thunderstorm, in which case you may avoid the worst winds by leaving it to port.

The best thing of all is to alter course so as to miss it. Where this is impracticable, take a precautionary reef, shut the hatch and clap on the oilskins.

If you see a cloud like this cumulonimbus, try to alter course to avoid it; these clouds often signal squally conditions and rain

193 GET THE GRIB

Are you looking for really sound wind and weather forecasting on your desktop, anywhere in the world, large area or small, with three-hour intervals and up to seven-day prognosis? We all are, aren't we? Well, here's a great solution and it's absolutely free.

Go to www.grib.us/ and download the software. Then follow the instructions and start to enjoy all the weather info you need, wherever you can access broadband. The data comes as a tiny email so it costs very little to receive, even if you're paying for Internet connectivity by the megabyte.

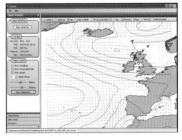

Weather GRIB files are very small so can be emailed

194   CYCLONIC

Here's a term we hear from time to time on the weather forecast.
But what does it mean? Cyclonic conditions are usually found in
the centre of a low pressure system away from any fronts. The
pressure is fairly static and is as low as it's going to get. There often
isn't a great deal of wind, although there may be, but one thing
is sure, no forecaster can tell us what its direction will be because
there are no isobars to define it. The sea is likely to be somewhat
confused as well, if the low is vigorous. Even so, if the forecast says
cyclonic, things could be worse. The weather's sure to be a lot less
pleasant out there in the isobars.

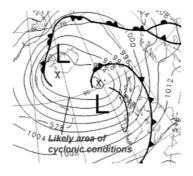

195   VERY POOR

You may hear the term 'very poor' creeping into the visibility
department of shipping forecasts. The Met Office website defines
this as 'less than 1 kilometre', which coincides with the old defini-
tion of fog. When quizzed, the Met Office said that fog remains
as it always has been and that the newer term could be cross-
referenced with it. Confused? So am I, but at least now we know
what they mean.

Is the visibility 'very poor' or is it 'foggy' – or both?

196 WATCH THE GLASS

It's all very well having the latest forecast from the radio, but sometimes a weather system winds up more than expected, as we all well know. Unless you have a barograph or one of the magic electronic equivalents, it pays to log the barometer every hour or so when it looks like trouble's brewing. Without being too pedantic about accuracy, if it falls 8 millibars in 3 hours you're almost certainly in for a full Force 8. Five millibars in the same time, and you'll soon be reefing down. Force 6 will be with you by the time the kettle boils. Sadly, the same applies to a rising glass, although the blow may not be with you for quite so long.

It pays to log the barometer

197 SEA FOG COOKING IN THE ISLANDS

The sort of fog caused by warm, moist air moving over colder water often clears up as you approach a shoreline with the wind blowing off it. This is because the air is dried as it passes across the warm land, and it's especially noticeable among islands.

Closing a weather shore in fog, you can have every hope that the air will clear before matters become critical. The Isle of Wight often leaves sharper visibility in the Solent than outside.

Jersey and Guernsey can work wonders, and on the comparatively rare occasions when sea fog drifts into Western Scotland, the coast is studded with islands capable of delivering a 'fog lee'.

Fog often clears in the lee of an island

198   A HEAVY HITTER

You can always tell if a squall is going to hit you by treating its extreme edges as if they were ships on potential collision headings. In other words, is it on a steady bearing?

One edge going ahead of you and one astern? It's got your number.

Both edges going the same way? Safe.

One edge missing and the other on a steady bearing? Take a chance with the oilies, but stand by the reefing tackle!

Treat storm clouds like ships – take bearings

199   FOG ON THE WAY

You'd think this photo was taken early in the morning before the mist has burned off, but it wasn't. Actually, it's teatime and a fog bank has just rolled in from the sea. The photographer was anchored next door. He'd been considering going out when his eyebrows suddenly became dewy. Then he felt his stowed mainsail; that was wet too, yet the day was still relatively clear. In fact, fog was teetering on the brink of forming, it just took a half-degree change of temperature to set it off.

Condensation in your eyebrows or on a woolly hat is a sure sign that fog is imminent. Another sign is a halo around your navigation lights at night.

If the conditions are right, a half-degree change in temperature can cause fog to form

200 PREDICT SEA BREEZE

Most of us know that on a calm, hot day along the coast, a sea breeze may well develop around lunchtime or even earlier. This happens when the land heats quicker than the sea and the air over it warms and rises, leaving cool air drawn in from the colder sea to fill the 'vacuum'. Predicting a sea breeze can be helped by watching the formation of fluffy cumulus clouds over the land. These indicate that the warm, moist air is starting to rise at the 'sea breeze front', and are a good indication that an onshore wind will follow. If the clouds start streaming out over the water, it means the upper air current is in that direction. This encourages formation of a circulating sea-breeze engine, which will probably make the breeze stronger. It can kick up to Force 6 in places, so keep a weather eye on the clouds.

Classic cloud on the sea-breeze front